The Shepherd's Fortune

Timeless Parables on Patience, Risk, and What Actually Grows

Eleanor Voss

First edition, 2026

Published by Eleanor Voss

Contents

FOREWORD

My grandmother Elspeth kept a lambing journal in pencil on the back of feed bills. I found it after she died, tucked inside a King James Bible she never read. February 19, 1962: *Twin ewes, one stillborn. Buried below the hawthorn.* March 3, 1964: *Ram broke fence. Found him two valleys over. Cost me a day.* April 12, 1967: *Sold six yearlings. Put half away. Spring always comes.*

That last line—*Spring always comes*—she'd underlined twice.

I didn't understand it then. I was seven, maybe eight, watching her move through morning chores with the kind of attention most people reserve for things they love. She didn't love the sheep, exactly. She respected them. There's a difference. Love makes you sentimental. Respect makes you careful.

She taught me to count lambs the way other kids learned to count money: as something that grows if you pay attention and vanishes if you don't. A ewe that lambs well for three seasons becomes the foundation of next year's flock. A ram that throws strong offspring is worth ten that look impressive at market. She knew which animals would survive a hard winter and which ones were borrowing time.

I'm supposed to tell you that this book will teach you timeless principles of wealth-building through the metaphor of shepherding. That the lessons of the hillside translate directly to your 401(k). That patience compounds, diversification protects, and long-term thinking wins.

All of that is true.

But—and I should say this now before you waste your time—what I actually learned from watching my grandmother wasn't about getting rich. It was about not being afraid. She kept those sheep because they were the difference between eating and not eating, between heating the house in January and burning furniture. The arithmetic of her life was that simple and that unforgiving. She didn't optimize. She survived.

And here's what I've noticed after twenty years of watching people chase financial independence: most of us are trying to build wealth the way my grandmother kept sheep, except we've never stood in a freezing barn at two in the morning pulling a breech lamb, never had to decide which animals to cull before winter because we can't feed them all. We're playing a high-stakes game with tools we don't understand and stakes we can't see.

You might be thinking: *Great, another book telling me money is actually about character and discipline and the long view. I've heard this.*

Fair.

But I'm not here to tell you to budget better or start a side hustle or invest in index funds—though I should say, I do all of those things, for what it's worth. I'm here because I spent a decade interviewing families who built quiet, multi-generational wealth, and almost none of them did it the way the personal finance books describe. They did it the way my grandmother kept sheep: by making small, unglamorous decisions over and over until the pattern became automatic. By knowing the difference between what compounds and what just looks good. By not panicking when the ram broke the fence.

The cost of not knowing this—really knowing it in your bones, not just as a concept—is that you spend your whole life optimizing for a future that never arrives. You save for retirement but you're too exhausted at sixty-five to enjoy it. You chase returns but you can't sleep because the market dropped. You teach your kids about wealth but they hear anxiety, not wisdom.

I watched my father do this. He read every book, followed every strategy, rebalanced quarterly. He retired at sixty-seven with a portfolio worth just over two million dollars and died at seventy-one having spent almost none of it. He was still afraid.

My grandmother, who never had more than thirty sheep at once, spent her last decade exactly as she pleased.

This book contains twenty-one parables set in a shepherd's valley—not because shepherding is romantic or because I think you should quit your job and raise livestock, but because the risks there are visible. A coin sits in your account doing nothing until you move it. A sheep gets sick, breaks a leg, wanders off, dies giving birth. You can't ignore it. You can't automate it. You have to learn to see what's actually happening, not what you wish were happening.

Some of these stories are mine. Some came from the families I interviewed—people who recognized their own lives in the first volume and sent me letters, called me, showed up at readings with stories their grandparents had told them. A woman in Perth described how her great-grandfather survived the Depression by trading lambs for flour, one transaction at a time, never accumulating enough to attract attention but never quite going under. A man in Nebraska told me about his mother's rule: never sell a breeding ewe in a panic, even when cash is tight. Both of those became parables.

I'm calling this a book about wealth because that's what people will search for. But—and to be honest, this is what I actually think—it's a book about stopping the noise in your head long enough to figure out what you're building toward and whether you actually want it.

Read these slowly. One per sitting, maybe. Let them sit. Some will land immediately. Some won't make sense until you're standing in your own version of that freezing barn, deciding what to keep and what to let go.

The shepherd in the first parable makes a choice between two flocks. That's where we'll start—not with principles or frameworks, but with a decision. Because that's where wealth actually begins: the moment you realize you're already choosing, whether you meant to or not.

INTRODUCTION

I spent three years writing a book about money I didn't follow myself.

The working title was something forgettable—*Building Wealth Through Discipline* or *The Seven Pillars of Financial Freedom*—and every chapter laid out a careful system for optimizing your path to prosperity. Budget templates. Investment timelines. Compound-interest calculators that showed you'd be a millionaire by sixty-five if you just stuck to the plan. I had spreadsheets. I had case studies. I had everything except peace of mind.

Because here's what I didn't write: the chapter about lying awake at 2 a.m. running scenarios. The one about turning down a trip with friends because it wasn't in the five-year forecast. The part where optimization starts to feel less like freedom and more like a very sophisticated cage.

I should probably tell you to ignore everything that book said. Though to be honest, some of it was fine. The problem wasn't the advice—it was the premise underneath it. That wealth-building is a game you can win if you're smart enough, disciplined enough, strategic enough. That the goal is to reach some finish line where you've finally accumulated enough to feel safe.

But I've watched people cross that line. I've seen the goalposts move.

There's a story—and I promise this one is real, not the kind of clean parable you find in most money books—about a shepherd in the Swiss Alps named Jakob Hutter. He lived in the 1500s, during a period when the land was being carved up and small farmers were being squeezed out by larger estates. Hutter had a modest flock, nothing impressive, but he made a decision that seemed insane to his neighbors: he started sharing his grazing land with shepherds who'd lost theirs.

Not renting it. Sharing it.

His wealthier neighbors thought he'd lost his mind. You don't give away competitive advantage. You don't weaken your position. But Hutter had done the math differently. He'd realized that a shepherd alone—even a wealthy one—was vulnerable in ways that a community of shepherds wasn't. When wolves came (and they always did), when winters were harsh (and they always were), the shepherds who survived weren't the ones with the most sheep. They were the ones other people would help.

This sounds noble until you remember that Hutter wasn't being altruistic—he was being terrified. He'd seen what happened to isolated wealth. It made you a target. It made you paranoid. It made you spend your best years guarding what you had instead of enjoying it.

I came across Hutter's story in an anthropology text, not a finance book, and it stopped me cold. Because I'd been writing about wealth accumulation as if it were purely a individual engineering problem—optimize your inputs, maximize your returns, secure your future. But Hutter understood something I'd missed: the real question isn't how much you can accumulate. It's how early you can stop being afraid.

And fear, it turns out, doesn't care about your net worth.

I know people with seven-figure portfolios who check their accounts three times a day. I know people with almost nothing who sleep fine. The difference isn't the number—it's whether they trust the ground under their feet. Whether they believe people will show up when things go wrong. Whether they've built something that can't be taken away by a market crash or a medical emergency or the ten thousand other things we can't control.

You might be thinking this sounds like I'm about to tell you money doesn't matter, that community is everything, that you should give away your savings and trust the universe. I'm not. Money matters. It buys real security, real options, real breathing room. I'm not romantic about poverty—I've been broke enough to know better.

But I am saying that most financial advice is solving the wrong problem. It's teaching you to build a bigger barn when what you actually need is to stop lying awake afraid the barn will burn down.

The chapters that follow aren't about accumulation. They're about the thing that comes before accumulation, the thing that makes wealth actually work: trust. Trust in other people, yes, but also trust in yourself—that you'll be okay even if the plan doesn't go perfectly. That you can make a decision that looks inefficient on paper and still be fine. That the goal isn't to optimize every variable but to reach the point where you don't have to.

Some of these chapters will feel like parables because that's how this stuff has been passed down for centuries—shepherds and flocks and valleys, the old language of resource and risk and community. But underneath the metaphor is something concrete: what it actually costs you to live in fear of money, and what becomes possible when you don't.

The first cost is time. How many years will you spend planning for a future you're too anxious to enjoy when it arrives?

ONE — The Two Flocks

I'm sitting in a Fidelity office in 2019 looking at two fund options—one that's returned 23% annually for three years running, the other that's averaged 7% for the last twenty—and the advisor is walking me through projected returns, and I can feel myself leaning toward the flashy one, the way you do when someone shows you a graph that goes up and to the right faster than you thought graphs were allowed to go. I didn't pick it. Though I should say, not because I was smart enough to know better in that moment, but because I'd already lived through the story I'm about to tell you, and it had cost me enough the first time that my hand wouldn't sign the paperwork even when my brain was trying to.

The story that stopped my hand that afternoon is about two shepherds in a valley I've never been to, told to me by someone who learned it from someone who learned it from someone, the way the best financial lessons always travel—not through whitepapers, but through the particular shame of watching someone you know lose everything because they believed a story that sounded too good to be the kind that ends badly.

There were two young shepherds in the valley the autumn old Ossian was still alive to remember it. Their names were Fen and Cael. Cousins. They inherited their flocks within a season of each other, and that's the whole of what they had in common.

The valley in those years kept its old custom of dividing inheritances strictly by bloodline rather than by need, which meant when Fen and Cael's grandmother died within a season of their grandfather, the flocks passed to them in almost exactly equal number and quality. Same grazing rights. Same stretch of hillside. Same starting point in every measurable sense a tally-keeper could record.

Ossian himself—already old by then, the kind of old where you've stopped being surprised by what people do and started being surprised when they don't do exactly what you expect—remarked at the funeral gathering that he'd rarely seen two young men begin so evenly matched. It would be, he said, an interesting thing to watch over the coming years. Interesting in the particular sense old men use the word when they already suspect how a story ends and are too polite to say it outright.

You need to picture them to understand what happened next. Cael was a year older and had always been the one who moved first. First to climb the tallest rock behind the house, first to court a girl at the summer fair, first to decide a thing was true before he'd fully tested it. Fen had grown up watching him do it, finding his own slower way to the same place a season or two later, learning something from the watching that Cael, moving too fast to look back, never learned himself. They'd been raised in the same low farmhouse after Fen's mother died young and his father sent him to live with his uncle's family rather than raise a boy alone on a hill farm. So they knew each other the way brothers do, which is to say they knew each other's patterns well enough to stop seeing them as choices and start seeing them as weather.

Fen's flock came from his grandmother. A stubborn hill breed with coarse grey wool and legs like fence posts. Ugly animals that matured slow and lambed light—one lamb per ewe most years, sometimes none. They were the kind of sheep that had walked that valley for longer than anyone could account for, bred for nothing except staying alive through what the mountain did to them each winter. His grandmother had told him, the winter before she died and left them to him, that a hill ewe was not bred to be admired. "She's bred to still be standing in the pasture the morning after the kind of night that isn't meant to be survived," the old woman said.

"Everything else about her is beside the point."

Cael's flock came from a trader.

The trader had walked up from the lowlands with a story about a southern breed—fat, quick-growing, twin-lambing, wool soft as a child's hair, worth three times what hill wool fetched at market, he said. The trader had a way of talking that made the whole valley feel, for the length of his visit, like a place that had been quietly missing out on something. He spread a fleece across his knee at the tavern for anyone who'd look. Softer than anything the valley's own sheep produced. Let men run it through their fingers and imagine what it might fetch. Cael sold half his grandfather's old flock to buy forty of the southern sheep, over the muttered objections of an uncle who thought the trader's prices for the old flock—paid quick and in coin—were suspiciously generous for animals the trader clearly meant to resell at a markup elsewhere.

Cael didn't hear the objection as a warning. He heard it as the kind of caution older men always offer younger ones, out of habit more than conviction, and set it aside.

Within the year he had lambs to sell that Fen, with his slow grey ewes, did not.

Here's what I need you to understand about that moment, because this is the moment where most of us make the choice that costs us the next ten years. Cael looked at his cousin's flock and saw something that was falling behind. Fen looked at his own flock and saw something that had survived another winter. They were looking at the same arithmetic. They were reaching opposite conclusions. And the valley, watching both of them, didn't yet know which conclusion would turn out to be the one that mattered.

"You'll be poor a long while yet," Cael told Fen at the shearing that spring. Not unkindly. The way you tell a man something you believe is simply true. "Mine will have doubled again by autumn." He said it with an arm around Fen's shoulders, the way he'd always spoken to his younger cousin—more instruction than boast, as though he were still the one showing Fen where the tallest rock behind the house was, still expecting Fen to find his own slower way there eventually.

Fen didn't argue it. He had nothing to argue with. His flock had grown by exactly the number the hill breed always grew by, which was not much, and his wool that year sold for a fair price and no more. He put what it earned toward a stone wall along the north edge of his pasture.

Cael thought it was a waste. "A wall doesn't lamb," he pointed out one afternoon, watching Fen haul stone up from the creek bed instead of walking to market with him.

Fen only shrugged and kept hauling. He didn't have a clever answer for it. He only had a feeling, inherited from a grandmother who'd never once explained herself further than she needed to, that the wall would matter more than it looked like it would.

You might be thinking, at this point, that you know how this story ends. The flashy investment crashes, the boring one wins, Fen was right all along, moral of the story is to be patient and boring and you'll be fine. That's not the lesson. I spent a decade thinking that was the lesson, and it cost me—to be honest—more than I want to admit in print, because I learned patience but not the thing that makes patience worth anything, which is knowing what you're being patient *for*. Fen wasn't being patient because patience is a virtue. He was building a wall because his grandmother had taught him that the mountain asks a question every winter, and the question is whether you built the thing that lets you survive the asking.

The southern sheep were, for two years, everything the trader had promised. They grew fat on the valley's good summer grass. They lambed twins. Cael's flock swelled the way water swells a stream after rain. He built a second byre to hold the overflow and talked, that second autumn, of leasing more pasture from a neighbor to make room for the growth he expected the third year to bring.

He built nothing to shelter them beyond what any ordinary summer required. He didn't need to. The flock itself was the wall, the reserve, the whole of his fortune, growing every season faster than any wall could. And for two winters—both of them mild by the valley's usual measure—he was not wrong.

The third winter came in hard and early. A fortnight before anyone expected it. The kind that closes the high passes overnight and buries the low pasture under snow too deep for grazing.

Fen had finished his wall the summer before, on nothing more than the same quiet feeling that had told him to start it, and had begun—without quite calling it by any name—keeping back a little more hay each autumn than the season strictly seemed to demand. Not because he expected trouble, but because the checking itself, done daily whether or not it was ever strictly needed, was the thing that let him notice trouble the moment it arrived rather than the week after.

The morning the storm broke, Fen walked his own pasture before dawn the way he did every winter morning. Checking the wall. Checking the flock. Checking the sky out of the same old habit his grandmother had drilled into him since boyhood. He found nothing wrong that first morning, or the second, or the third.

It was on the fourth morning, walking the fence line with his dogs, that he first heard it—carried faint on the wind from the direction of Cael's farm—the particular high, distressed sound of sheep that have been cold too long. A sound every shepherd in the valley learns to recognize early and dreads hearing on someone else's land, because it means the trouble has already gone on longer than it should have before anyone thought to ask for help.

Fen's grey ewes had wintered in worse. They pawed through the snow to the grass beneath it, the way the breed always had, the way it had been bred to for longer than memory holds. He lost four animals that winter. Old ones. He counted it an ordinary loss.

Cael's southern sheep had never seen snow like it. They didn't know how to find grass beneath what they'd never had to find grass beneath before. They stood at the fences and did not paw.

He fed them what hay he had, which was not enough, because a flock bred to grow fast had never taught him to store slow. He had spent two mild winters believing the flock's own growth was reserve enough against anything the mountain could ask of it. By the second week he was walking the fence line at night with a lantern, watching animals stand shivering in drifts they didn't know how to move through. By the third week he had begun making the trip to Fen's farm before dawn. Ashamed. To ask whether there was hay to spare.

Fen gave what he could. Not out of any wish to be proven right in front of his cousin—which brought him no pleasure at all—but because the wall he'd built the summer before had space enough behind it to shelter a few of Cael's weakest animals along with his own, and he made that space without being asked twice.

It was not enough to save the flock. It was enough, Cael said later, to keep him from losing every animal he owned in a single season.

And he never forgot which cousin had opened his gate to him at four in the morning with no complaint in his voice at all.

By the thaw Cael had lost better than half of the southern flock. The half that lived had lambed poorly, weakened by a winter their bodies had no answer for. The wool the survivors gave that spring was thin and short-stapled, worth less at market than even Fen's coarse grey clip, because an animal that has spent a winter simply trying to stay alive has little left over to grow good fleece with.

Here's the part of the story that doesn't get told enough, the part I didn't understand until I'd lost my own flock—not sheep, but the portfolio I'd built in my thirties on three consecutive years of tech stocks that felt, at the time, like the thing everyone else was missing and I'd been smart enough to catch. The loss itself is the obvious lesson. The thing that actually matters is what the loss *costs you that you can't get back.*

Cael lost half his flock. That's the number everyone remembers. What he actually lost was three years. The three years it took him to rebuild what he'd had before the trader walked up from the lowlands. He was twenty-six when he bought the southern sheep. He was twenty-nine, almost thirty, when he finally had a flock the size of the one he'd inherited, and by then Fen's flock—grown slowly, compounded quietly, never flashy, never fast—was twice the size of Cael's and throwing off enough surplus wool each year that Fen had begun buying pasture from neighbors instead of leasing it.

Three years is what it costs you to learn the lesson the hard way. Three years you don't get back. Three years of your late twenties, which are—I'm just telling you what I learned too late to use—the only years you have when you're still young enough to recover from a wipeout but old enough to make the recovery count for something.

Spend those years rebuilding from zero and you're not starting over from where you were. You're starting over from where you could have been if you'd built the wall first.

Word of Cael's losses spread through the valley that spring the way such news always does. More than one household found itself, without much discussion, quietly re-examining its own reserves against the possibility of a winter arriving early again. A small ripple of caution that the valley's tally-keeper noted, in the records that year, as an uptick in stored hay across nearly every farm—though none of the shepherds involved would likely have named Cael's flock as their reason if asked directly.

This is how a valley actually learns most of its hardest lessons. Not through any single dramatic sermon, but through a hundred quiet households watching a neighbor's misfortune and adjusting, a little, without ever needing to say why.

Fen's wall, that spring, was finished. It kept his weakest ewes penned close to the house through the worst nights of lambing, out of the wind that had, in years past, killed newborns by the dozen. He lost almost none. His flock—grey and coarse and slow—had grown, in the plain unglamorous way it always grew, into something Cael's could no longer catch. Not because Fen had done anything dramatic in three years, but because he had done the same small, patient thing three years running, while Cael had done something spectacular for two of them and then lost most of it in a fortnight.

There was a period, that terrible month between the storm's passing and the full accounting of what remained, when Cael did not come to Fen's farm at all. He stayed in his own half-empty byre among the animals that were left, unable to face the arithmetic of what the winter had done or the cousin who had, without meaning to, provided the arithmetic's counterexample standing in plain view across the valley.

His wife—a patient woman named Eithne who had married him in the second of the two good years and watched the third undo most of what she'd married into—was the one who finally walked him over to Fen's gate, more or less by the elbow. She told him plainly that shame was a poor excuse for losing a cousin on top of everything else the winter had already cost him.

Cael did not resent him for it, in the end. He came to Fen's farm again that spring, once the snow had cleared enough for walking. Not for hay this time, but simply to sit on the wall he'd once called useless and admit, out loud, that he'd been wrong about what it was for.

"I thought you were building a fence," he said. "You were building the only thing that mattered."

He sold what remained of the southern flock. Bought hill ewes with what the sale brought him. Started again the slow way, the way his grandfather had, the way the valley had always demanded whether or not a trader ever walked up from the lowlands to say otherwise. He built his own wall the very first summer, before he'd so much as doubled his new flock once, and told anyone who asked that he was simply doing what his cousin had already proven, at no small cost to himself, was worth doing first.

I should tell you what I actually did with this story, because the lesson I just gave you—build the wall first, choose what survives over what grows fast, all of that—is the lesson I tell people when they ask for advice. It is not the lesson I followed the first time I had money to invest.

I bought the flashy fund. The one that had returned 23% annually for three years. I bought it in late 2019, rode it up for six more months, watched it crater in March 2020, sold near the bottom because I was terrified it would go lower, and spent the next two years rebuilding what I'd lost while the boring fund—the 7% one I'd passed on—compounded quietly upward and left me so far behind that I didn't catch up until 2024. I lost two years. Not money. Time. The two years between thirty-three and thirty-five when I should have been building momentum and was instead clawing back to even.

The second time—the Fidelity office in 2019 I mentioned at the start, which was actually 2021, I lied about the year because I was embarrassed to admit I nearly made the same mistake twice in two years—the second time, I picked the boring one. Not because I'm smarter now, but because I'd already paid full tuition for the lesson and didn't want to pay it again.

Here's what you do with this on Monday morning, because a story about sheep is useless to you if it doesn't tell you what to do with your own flock.

Open your investment account. Look at what you own. Ask yourself, for each position, whether it's a hill ewe or a southern sheep. A hill ewe is the thing that will still be standing in your portfolio the morning after the kind of night that isn't meant to be survived. A southern sheep is the thing that grows fast when conditions are perfect and dies when they're not. You probably own both. Everyone does. The question is which one you're adding to when you have new money to invest.

If you're adding to the southern sheep because they've been growing faster, I'm not going to tell you you're wrong. Cael wasn't wrong for two years. I wasn't wrong for six months. You might not be wrong for longer than that. But I am telling you that the mountain asks a question every winter, and the question is whether you built the thing that lets you survive the asking, and if the answer is no, you will lose more than money. You'll lose the time it takes to rebuild it, and time is the only part of your fortune you can't buy back at any price.

The wall comes first. Always. Even when it looks like a waste. Even when your cousin is doubling his flock while you're hauling stone. Especially then.

I told the story of Fen and Cael for years before I understood that its true ending wasn't the wall or the winter at all, but the two cousins sitting together on that same stone wall decades later, old men by then, telling the story themselves to their own grandchildren exactly the way I am telling it to you now. Which is, I think, the surest sign a story has earned its place in a valley's memory.

The next story is harder to tell well, because its lesson is not about patience but about its opposite cousin—the wager—and how easily the two can be mistaken for each other by someone who has been patient for a very long time and is starting to wonder whether patience was just another word for being afraid.

TWO — The Pass Before the Storm

Mera stood at the gate that morning and watched her husband disappear into the pre-dawn grey with their entire flock. All of it. Every sheep they owned moving in one long line toward the high pass.

She'd said nothing to stop him.

That's the part I keep coming back to when I think about this story—not Torin's decision, but Mera's silence. Because she *knew*. The way you know when you're about to make a financial decision that sounds perfectly reasonable in the moment but sits wrong in your gut. The way you know when someone's talking you into something that makes sense on paper but violates every instinct you've developed over years of watching what actually happens versus what people say will happen.

Three clear mornings. That's what Torin had said at breakfast, his voice carrying that particular confidence of a man who's done his homework. "Three clear mornings in a row—when have we ever seen that in late summer? The weather's holding. The meadow on the far side is untouched, and if we wait another week, someone else will get there first."

Mera had nodded. Poured him more tea. Said something about checking the gate latches.

What she didn't say: *My grandfather told me about three clear mornings once. He said they're the mountain's way of making you comfortable right before it stops being polite.*

But who wants to be the person who brings up their grandfather's folklore when your husband is laying out a plan that actually makes sense? Torin wasn't reckless. Twenty years they'd been building this flock—twenty years of the kind of patience that makes your neighbors think you're too cautious, too slow, missing opportunities while you count and recount what you already have.

And maybe that's exactly why this decision felt different to him. Maybe after two decades of being the careful one, he'd earned the right to take one calculated risk.

Except—and I should say this plainly because I've done the exact same thing Torin did—there's a particular kind of dangerous thinking that happens when you've been cautious for a long time. You start to believe your caution has been building up like credits in an account. Like the universe owes you one. Like all those years of saying no to risky opportunities mean you've somehow purchased the right to one big yes without consequences.

It doesn't work that way.

Mera knew it didn't work that way. But she also knew what it felt like to watch someone you love finally reach for something after years of holding back. So she stood at the gate and watched the last of the sheep disappear into the grey, and then she walked back to the house and tried to convince herself that three clear mornings might actually mean three clear mornings.

The first day passed without incident. Word came back through Ewan, Torin's head shepherd, who'd stayed behind to manage the property: the flock was moving well, the pass was clear, Torin was making better time than expected.

The second day brought more of the same. The valley buzzed with the news—Torin's crossing the entire flock through in one push, the weather's holding, looks like he timed it perfectly.

Mera spent both days working through her normal routines with a knot in her stomach that wouldn't loosen. She mucked out the near paddock. Repaired a section of fence that didn't really need repairing. Reorganized the storage shed. Anything to keep her hands busy while her mind ran through scenarios she couldn't control.

On the third morning, she walked up to the low rise where Torin usually went for his early observations of the weather. The sky was still clear. Still that same deceptive blue that had held for three days now.

Four days, technically. Four mornings of absolute clarity.

She found herself thinking about Old Ossian. He'd stopped by six days earlier—just a visit, nothing formal, the way neighbors do when they've known each other for decades. He'd accepted tea, asked about the flock, listened to Torin's plan for the crossing.

"Send half," he'd said finally. Not as advice, exactly. More like he was describing what the weather looked like. Just a statement of fact.

Torin had bristled. Politely, but Mera knew that particular stiffness in his shoulders. "With respect, Ossian, I've been watching this pattern for two weeks. The conditions are as good as they're going to get. If I split the flock, I'm making two dangerous crossings instead of one."

Ossian had nodded slowly, the way old men do when they've said what they came to say and won't waste energy arguing. "That's one way to see it."

He'd left shortly after. Mera had wanted to ask him what the other way to see it was, but Torin was already moving on to other preparations, and the moment passed.

Now, standing on the rise with the valley spread out below her and the mountains looming above, she understood what Ossian meant.

Two crossings meant two separate risks, yes. But it also meant that if the weather turned—*when* the weather turned, because it always turned eventually—you'd lose half instead of everything.

It wasn't about the math of risk. It was about the math of survival.

Though I should be honest here: I'm describing this as if Mera had it all figured out on that third morning, standing on the rise with perfect clarity about probability and loss mitigation. She didn't. What she had was a feeling. The same feeling you get when you're about to put all your money into one investment because the timing seems perfect and everyone's saying it's a sure thing and you've been so careful for so long that this one big move feels almost... owed to you.

That feeling is your brain trying to get your attention.

Mera's brain was screaming. But Torin was already on the far side of the pass with their entire livelihood strung out behind him, so what exactly was she supposed to do with that feeling now?

The wind changed in the early afternoon of the third day.

Not dramatically. Just a shift—the air that had been still and warm all morning suddenly carrying a cold edge from the north. The kind of cold that doesn't belong in late summer. The kind that makes you look up at the sky even though the sky still looks perfectly clear.

Mera was in the garden when she felt it. She straightened up from the bean rows and turned her face toward the mountains, toward the pass where Torin and the flock would be beginning their descent if everything was going according to plan.

The sky above the peaks had changed. Not dark—nothing dramatic or obviously threatening. Just a thin haze of cloud beginning to gather along the ridgeline. Wispy. Almost delicate.

She watched those clouds for twenty minutes. Watched them thicken and multiply. Watched them begin their slow crawl down the shoulder of the mountain.

By evening, the first rain started. Light at first. Then steady. Then heavy enough that she could barely see the fence line from the kitchen window.

The wind picked up after dark—not the summer wind that blows warm and restless through the valley, but the autumn wind that comes down from the high peaks carrying winter's first warning. It bent the trees and rattled the shutters and turned the rain into something that sounded like handfuls of gravel being thrown against the walls.

Mera sat at the kitchen table and did not let herself imagine what that wind was doing in the pass. What it was doing to a flock of sheep with nowhere to shelter. What it was doing to a man who'd been so certain that three clear mornings meant the mountain had given its permission.

I want to tell you that she stayed calm. That years of experience had taught her how to wait through a storm without letting fear take over.

But that's not what happened. What happened is that Mera sat at that table with her hands wrapped around a mug of tea that went cold while she wasn't paying attention, and she made bargains with God and the mountain and anyone else who might be listening. She promised that if Torin came back safe, she'd never again keep silent when she knew something was wrong. She promised she'd speak up next time, even if it meant being the voice of caution everyone rolls their eyes at.

She was still sitting there when dawn broke grey and exhausted over the valley. The rain had stopped sometime in the last hour, leaving behind that particular stillness that comes after a storm has worn itself out.

Mera stood at the gate again. Waiting.

They came down from the pass just after sunrise. Torin in front, moving like a man who'd aged a decade overnight. The flock behind him, bedraggled and smaller than it should have been.

Mera counted them as they came through the gate. She couldn't help it. It's what you do when you've spent twenty years building something—you count what's left after the storm.

Seventy-three sheep made it back. They'd started with ninety-eight.

Twenty-five lost. In one night. Because the weather had looked clear and the opportunity had looked perfect and Torin had believed that caution could be stored up and spent like currency.

He didn't say anything as he came through the gate. Just looked at her with eyes that had seen the cost of his calculation, and she looked back with eyes that had known the cost before he'd left but hadn't found the words to make him understand.

Ewan appeared an hour later, exhausted and mud-covered. He told them what had happened in the pass: the storm had hit just as they'd reached the narrowest section, where the trail ran along a steep drop and there was nowhere to shelter. The sheep had panicked. Some had bolted over the edge. Others had simply given up in the cold and the wind and couldn't be roused to keep moving.

"We saved what we could," Ewan said quietly. "Torin kept them moving forward. If he'd stopped to try to save every one that went down, we'd have lost them all."

Mera nodded. Made tea. Set out food that no one had the stomach to eat.

What she was thinking: *We kept seventy-three because we risked ninety-eight. If we'd sent half, we'd have kept ninety-something.*

What she said: nothing.

Not because she didn't want to make Torin feel worse—though she didn't—but because there was nothing to say that the numbers hadn't already said for her. Twenty-five dead sheep are a very specific kind of education. The kind you can't argue with or contextualize or reframe as a learning experience.

You just have to sit with what they cost.

I think about Mera and Torin more than I probably should. Their story isn't just about sheep and mountains and weather that turned without warning. It's about every time we convince ourselves that careful preparation means we've eliminated risk instead of just managing it. Every time we decide that because we've been responsible for so long, we've earned the right to one big leap without consequences.

Here's what I actually believe, though I know it's not the advice you're supposed to give: there's no such thing as earning the right to ignore risk. Caution doesn't accumulate. The universe doesn't owe you one. And every single time you tell yourself that this time is different, that you've done your homework and the timing is perfect and you can't afford to miss this opportunity—you're one step closer to standing at a gate counting what came back instead of what you started with.

But—and I should be honest about this too—I've been Torin. I've looked at three clear mornings and convinced myself they meant permission instead of just weather. I've made the all-in move because I was tired of being the careful one and wanted to finally be the person who seized the moment.

The question isn't whether you'll be tempted to do what Torin did. You will. The question is whether you'll have a Mera in your life who knows better and whether you'll listen to her before you commit the whole flock.

Or—harder still—whether you'll be your own Mera. Whether you'll speak up when your gut knows something your spreadsheet doesn't. Whether you'll have the courage to be the cautious one even when caution looks like cowardice to everyone else watching.

Three months after the storm, Mera and Torin sat down and did something they'd never done before: they wrote down rules for how they'd make decisions about the flock.

Not goals. Not aspirations. Rules.

Rule one: Never move more than half the flock through any single point of risk, no matter how good the conditions look.

Rule two: When someone with more experience offers unsolicited caution, ask them what they're seeing that you're not.

Rule three: Clear weather doesn't mean safe weather. It means you can see what's coming before it arrives.

They posted these rules on the wall of their kitchen where they'd see them every morning. Not as a reminder of the storm—they didn't need a reminder of that—but as a guard against the story they'd inevitably start telling themselves as the years passed and the loss began to feel distant.

Because here's what happens with hard lessons: they fade. The pain gets softer. The numbers become abstract again. You start to think about all the opportunities you've passed up by being too cautious, and you forget what it felt like to count what came back through the gate.

The rules on the wall were their way of saying: we will not forget the cost of forgetting.

So what does this mean for you? What are you supposed to do with a story about sheep and storms and a man who risked everything because the timing looked perfect?

I could tell you to diversify. Split your risk. Keep something in reserve. All true. All correct. All the kind of advice that sounds perfectly sensible when you're reading it and perfectly insufficient when you're standing at the gate deciding what to do.

Because the real question isn't about tactics. It's about whether you're capable of hearing the warning before you need it.

Are you listening to your own gut when it tells you something feels wrong even though the numbers say it's right? Are you paying attention to the people who've lived through more storms than you have, even when their caution sounds like fear? Are you honest enough to admit when you're making a decision not because it's smart but because you're tired of being careful and you want permission to finally go for it?

Torin wasn't stupid. He was experienced, prepared, and rational. He just wanted one thing—this one crossing, this one opportunity—badly enough that he stopped seeing what Mera and Ossian saw clearly.

The mountain doesn't care how careful you've been. It doesn't grade on a curve. It just does what it does, and you either planned for it or you didn't.

Twenty-five sheep. That's what three clear mornings cost.

What are yours?

THREE — The Wool That Stayed

I was nineteen when I watched a woman stand at a market stall and talk herself out of buying the one thing she'd wanted for six years. She held the cloth up to the light. Ran her thumb across the weave. Asked the merchant three different questions about where it came from and whether the dye would hold. Then set it back down, thanked him, and walked away to buy a lamb instead.

Her name was Ide. Her sister Sorcha was standing next to me when it happened, and I watched Sorcha's face do something complicated—half affection, half exasperation, and maybe a third thing underneath that looked, if I'm honest about it, like the specific sadness of watching someone you love deny themselves pleasure for reasons you don't entirely understand and aren't sure you want to.

"She'll never buy it," Sorcha said, not quite to me. "She'll think about it all winter and convince herself she doesn't need it."

She was right. Ide never bought the cloth. But eleven years later, Ide built a stone house with a slate roof, and Sorcha was still living in the turf cottage their mother had left them. Same flock size. Same market. Same wool prices, near enough. The difference wasn't the wool. It was what each sister did with the coin the wool became, and I've been thinking about that difference ever since—not because one sister was right and the other wrong, but because most of us spend our whole lives negotiating between the two of them without ever quite naming the negotiation out loud.

Their father had died at sea when both girls were small. Lost with two other valley men on a trading voyage no one in the family talked about much afterward—one of those family silences that gets heavier the longer it sits. Their mother raised them alone on a modest flock with the kind of fierce, uncomplaining competence that doesn't announce itself but gets absorbed anyway, the way children absorb everything their parents do more than anything their parents say. She used to tell them, on the long winter evenings when there was nothing else to do but talk, that a woman raising children alone learns fast which kind of coin keeps a household fed through a bad year and which kind only makes a good year feel a little better while it lasts. She said both kinds mattered. She said the trouble came when a household forgot it needed both in the right proportion.

I don't know if either daughter understood what she meant at the time. I'm not sure their mother entirely understood it herself—it was the kind of thing you say because your own life has taught it to you in ways you can't quite translate into advice. But they split their mother's flock evenly when she died, down to the animal, each sister taking exactly half so neither could ever say the other had started ahead. Ide was the elder by two years. Quiet where Sorcha was quick to laugh. The kind of girl who'd sit an entire afternoon watching a spider finish a web rather than go looking for something more immediately entertaining. Sorcha had never sat still through the whole of anything if there was music or company to be had instead.

Their mother used to say Ide saved things without knowing she was saving them and Sorcha spent things without knowing she was spending them, and that the valley would eventually teach each of them what the other already understood by instinct. She didn't live to see whether it did.

The valley fair was the high point of the season for most households back then—still is, though it's gotten bigger and louder and a little less itself over the years. Three days of trading, music, and company that broke the long isolation of a shepherd's ordinary working life. No one in the valley, Ide least of all, ever thought

Sorcha wrong to love it the way she did. Sorcha took her share to the fair the same week it sold and came home light-handed and happy. A length of dyed cloth. A good knife. Sweets for her children. Once—this was year four or five—a fiddle she'd wanted since she was a girl, watched other families' children play at every fair for a decade before she finally had coin enough of her own, free and clear, to buy one without asking anyone's permission.

"Wool is meant to be worn on someone's back or heard in someone's music," she liked to say. "Not hidden in a jar."

There was a joy in her that Ide, watching, sometimes envied. A lightness that came, Ide privately suspected, precisely from never holding a coin long enough to feel its weight turn into worry. Sorcha's children grew up knowing the sound of their mother's fiddle on winter evenings. Knowing, too, that a good year at market meant a good week at the fair, cause and effect as plain and immediate as weather.

Ide took her share and did something that looked, to anyone watching, like nothing at all.

She bought a ewe most years. Sometimes two. Sometimes, in a lean year, none. She mended her own roof herself rather than pay to have it done—three cold weekends each autumn on a ladder with a mouthful of nails rather than a single afternoon's coin. She wore the same shawl to market for six years past when Sorcha would have replaced it, until the wool had gone thin at the elbows and the dye had faded to a color that no longer had a proper name. People in the valley didn't think of Ide as prospering. They thought of her as careful, which in a young woman wasn't always meant as a compliment. More than one neighbor wondered aloud, within her hearing, whether she meant to enjoy any of her own good fortune before she was too old to.

Here's what I should tell you, though I'm not sure I knew it clearly enough to say it at the time: a ewe bought in year one is not a ewe. It's a lineage.

By year four Ide's first ewe had lambed three times. By year seven its daughters had lambed. By year eleven, the single ewe Ide bought with her first spare coin had become, through nothing more dramatic than ordinary lambing season after ordinary lambing season, nineteen animals. Nineteen animals that had cost her, in truth, almost nothing beyond that first year's patience, because each one had paid for the next, quietly, the way interest pays for itself without ever asking to be noticed doing it.

Ide herself, if you'd pressed her, couldn't have told you the exact year any of the nineteen had been born. She'd simply stopped counting the small additions one by one and started, somewhere around year seven, counting the flock as a single growing thing instead.

Sorcha's fiddle sat in the corner of the cottage, beautiful and silent most of the year. It had given her joy in the moment of its buying and very little wealth in any of the moments since.

This is not—and I want to be careful here because the valley still tells this story wrong half the time—a story that condemns the fiddle. Sorcha's children remember their mother's music. That's its own kind of fortune. No one should tell you it isn't. To be honest, I've spent enough years now watching people deny themselves every small pleasure in the name of some future security they never quite reach to know that Sorcha's choice was, in its own way, braver than Ide's. It's easy to save. It's harder to decide, in the face of a whole valley's judgment about what a responsible woman ought to do with her coin, that you're going to buy the fiddle anyway and let the future sort itself out.

But the stone house went up on Ide's land, not Sorcha's.

The builders who raised it that spring were some of the same men who'd helped Sorcha's husband thatch their family's roof years earlier, with coin from an especially good wool year. One of them remarked to Ide, partway through the work, that he'd watched her save toward this house for so many small seasons running he'd half assumed she'd simply decided never to build it at all—content instead to let the coin keep quietly multiplying on its own.

She told him only that the house had always been coming, in its own time. That a thing worth having rarely announced itself loudly in the years before it arrived.

The house went up because nineteen sheep, sold down carefully over three seasons, could buy slate and stone in a way eleven years of small, immediate pleasures never could. What Ide had discovered—without ever naming it so plainly—was that wool spent the week it arrives buys only that week's pleasure, however real. Wool set aside to grow buys, eventually, something that doesn't need buying twice.

There's a third character in this story who rarely gets mentioned when it's told at the fair, and that's Sorcha's eldest daughter, Niamh. She grew up watching both her mother's joyful spending and her aunt's quiet accumulating with the particular clear-eyed attention of a child deciding, without yet knowing she was deciding it, which household she meant to build when she was grown.

She loved her mother's fiddle evenings without reservation. They were, she said later, some of the happiest memories of her childhood.

But she also noticed—the way children notice things adults assume are invisible to them—that her aunt Ide never seemed anxious about a hard season the way her own mother sometimes did. Never had to choose, in a lean year, between mending the roof and feeding the children, because the choice had already been made, quietly, years before the lean year arrived.

When Niamh married and took her own small flock into the world, she built it the way her aunt had. One careful ewe at a time. She told her mother, with the specific gentleness a daughter reserves for a parent she loves without wanting to become, that she'd simply decided to enjoy her fiddle evenings after the wall was built rather than before it.

Sorcha watched the house rise stone by stone that spring with a feeling she had trouble putting a name to at first. Then one evening, sitting with her fiddle silent in her lap for once, she recognized it plainly as something closer to grief than envy. Not for the house itself, which she'd never much wanted. For the eleven winters of coin she could no longer quite account for. Spent well and joyfully in the moment, and gone now as completely as if they'd never been earned at all.

She said as much to Ide one evening, half-joking, half not. Ide—who had never once in eleven years said a critical word about her sister's fiddle or her sister's fair-days or her sister's children's sweets—only shook her head and told her plainly that she'd envied Sorcha's lightness every single one of those eleven years. That a house with no music in it, and no children who remembered their mother dancing, would have been a poor kind of wealth on its own.

The sisters remained close their whole lives. Ide, once the stone house stood finished, gave Sorcha a room in it for as long as she wanted one. Sorcha took it, laughing, and brought her fiddle, and played it most winter evenings in a kitchen with a slate roof over it that would outlast them both. Neither sister, in all the years after, ever suggested that the other should have lived any differently than she had.

Here's what I've come to understand about that story, all these years later: the part that matters isn't which sister was right. It's that most of us are living some version of this argument right now, this week, without naming it clearly enough to decide it on purpose.

You might be thinking—I would have been thinking this at nineteen—that the moral here is obvious. Save like Ide. Delay gratification. Build the flock. But I've watched enough people save themselves into lonely, joyless old age to know that's not the whole answer either. The real question isn't whether to be Ide or Sorcha. It's whether you know, right now, which one you've been, and whether that's still the choice you mean to be making.

Because here's what happens if you don't choose on purpose: the years choose for you. And the years, left to themselves, will spend your coin on whatever's easiest in the moment—which is almost never the thing you'd choose if you sat down once a year and asked yourself honestly what you're building toward and whether this week's spending is building it or borrowing from it.

I'm not going to tell you there's a perfect ratio. Their mother said both kinds of coin mattered, and I think she was right, though I also think she didn't live long enough to tell them what the right proportion actually looked like in practice. Maybe there isn't one. Maybe it's different for every household, every temperament, every stage of life.

But I can tell you this: if you don't know, right now, how much of your coin is staying and how much is leaving, you're not making a choice. You're just hoping it works out. And hope, however necessary, is not a plan.

So here's the thing you can do Monday, or this week, or as soon as you set this book down: sit down with your accounts—doesn't matter if it's a ledger or a jar or a banking app that intimidates you—and divide last month's coin into two categories. Not income and expenses. That's not the division that matters here. Divide it into *the coin that became something that keeps growing* and *the coin that became a single moment's pleasure and then was gone*. Don't judge either category yet. Just see them clearly.

Most people, when they do this for the first time, discover they've been Sorcha without meaning to be. That almost all of it left, and almost none of it stayed. That's not a moral failing. It's just information. But it's information you can't act on until you see it plainly, the way Sorcha finally saw it the spring Ide's house went up—and by then eleven winters had already passed, and the choice was mostly already made.

The other thing people discover, almost as often, is that they've been Ide without ever quite admitting it to themselves. That they've saved so carefully for so long they've forgotten what they were saving for, and the fiddle they wanted six years ago is still sitting in the merchant's stall because they've talked themselves into believing they don't need it, or don't deserve it, or can't afford it even though the numbers say otherwise. And that's its own kind of poverty—the kind that builds a stone house with no music in it and wonders, twenty years later, why the walls feel cold.

I don't know which one you are. But I'd bet a year's wool you know, or you will as soon as you look.

The sisters' story doesn't end with the house. It ends with Niamh, the daughter who watched both lives and chose deliberately between them. That's the part I keep coming back to. Not that Ide was right or Sorcha was wrong, but that Niamh saw both paths clearly enough to choose one on purpose instead of drifting into it by accident. She knew what the fiddle had cost her mother, and she knew what the waiting had cost her aunt, and she decided—young enough that the decision would compound for decades, the way Ide's first ewe had compounded into nineteen—that she wanted the wall first and the music after.

You don't have to make Niamh's choice. But you do have to make *a* choice, and you have to make it before the years make it for you. Because the wool will sell, and the coin will come, and it will go somewhere. The only question is whether you're the one deciding where, or whether you're just watching it leave and hoping, eleven years from now, that it went somewhere that mattered.

What arrives fast and leaves fast has done its work the moment it's gone. What stays, even when you forget it's there, keeps working long after you've stopped thinking about it. Quietly becoming more of itself while you sleep, while you shear, while you live your life around it. The coin itself doesn't care which path it takes.

But the wall you haven't built yet does.

FOUR — The Honest Scale

I'm supposed to tell you that reputation is everything in business, that you should guard it carefully, build it slowly, never take shortcuts that might damage it. That's the responsible advice.

Though I should say—to be honest—the first time I had a chance to shortchange someone and get away with it cleanly, I nearly took it. I was twenty-three, freelancing, desperately broke, and a client had overpaid me by mistake, a full invoice's worth, and I sat there at my kitchen table for probably twenty minutes with my finger hovering over the "refund" button thinking about whether anyone would ever actually notice. I sent it back eventually, but not because I was especially noble about it. I was just terrified of being the kind of person who wouldn't.

That fear—not nobility, just plain fear of becoming someone I'd hate—has kept me more honest over the years than any amount of moralizing ever did. Which is why I keep coming back to this story, the one about the two wool traders who walked the valley in those years. Both of them weighed what they bought on scales. Only one of them weighed true.

*

Traders were, in that country and that era, a necessary but only ever half-trusted part of the valley's yearly rhythm. They walked in each shearing season from the lowlands or the market towns beyond the pass, bought what the flocks had produced, and walked out again with it, returning the following year or not depending on where the trade routes carried them. A shepherd rarely had the means to haul wool to a distant market himself—not when the flock demanded everything else a season had to give—and so the relationship between valley and trader was, of necessity, one of trust extended to relative strangers year after year, with almost no recourse if that trust was ever quietly abused.

It is, Maren always said, exactly the kind of relationship most likely to reward a patient cheat. And exactly the kind of relationship this story exists to warn against trusting on reputation alone, no matter how pleasant that reputation sounds when it walks through your door smiling.

The dishonest one—his name is not remembered, or perhaps was never asked, which tells you something on its own—kept a scale with a thumb's worth of give built into its balance. So slight that a shepherd checking his own math afterward would blame his counting before he'd blame the scale.

He had a pleasant, unhurried manner about him. The kind that put shepherds at ease and made them feel foolish for the impulse, when it came, to double-check his arithmetic in front of him. He never rushed a transaction. He'd sit at a kitchen table, drink the tea he was offered, ask after a man's father or a woman's flock, and weigh the wool slowly, almost ceremonially, as though the care he took with the physical act of measuring proved something about his character. It didn't. But it looked like it did, and that was the whole game.

It was a difficult thing to catch him at even for a shepherd actively suspicious, since the shortfall on any single fleece rarely amounted to more than a man might reasonably attribute to his own imprecise counting at home. The trader was careful—genuinely, methodically careful—never to let his margin grow so large in any single transaction that it became worth a shepherd's while to make a fuss over. He paid a little less than fair for every fleece he bought. Made his margin on the difference. Moved on to the next valley before anyone had counted closely enough to notice.

It was, in its way, a patient kind of dishonesty. Never so much off the true weight that any single shepherd felt robbed, only ever enough that the trader's own margin quietly outpaced what an honest scale would have allowed him, season after season, valley after valley, a thumb's weight at a time.

You might be thinking this sounds almost victimless, the way I'm describing it. A little off the top, barely noticeable, nobody really hurt. That's exactly what the trader thought too, right up until the moment the valley stopped selling to him entirely and he had to find new ground. But I'm getting ahead of myself, because the cost of this—what it actually took from him, not in moral terms but in plain economic ones—only becomes visible when you set it next to what the honest trader built instead.

*

Bryde had come to the trade unusually for a woman of that country and that era. She'd inherited the business from an uncle who had no sons of his own and had taught her the scales the way he might have taught a nephew, insisting from her earliest days in the trade that a trader's whole worth lay in the two things a customer could never fully verify themselves: the honesty of the weight and the fairness of the price offered against it.

"Anyone can learn to buy wool," he told her once, when she was still a girl following him on his rounds, her feet blistering in boots too big for her because she'd grown into them yet. "Only a few ever learn to be believed while doing it. And belief—" he tapped the scale with one finger, the way you'd tap a lesson into someone's skull, "—belief is the only thing in this trade that actually compounds."

She took that to heart in a way most people don't take advice to heart, which is to say she made it expensive for herself to follow. Every single spring, before the season began, she walked her scale to the market town—a half-day's journey out of her way—and paid a fee to have it checked against the town standard. Her own cost. Her own time. Before she'd bought a single fleece that season. Just to be certain the numbers she gave a shepherd were the true numbers and not merely numbers that felt true.

She paid what wool was worth. Some years that meant she made less on a transaction than the dishonest trader made on the same fleece from the same shepherd. She knew this. She did it anyway.

A younger trader once asked her, half in jest, whether it wasn't a foolish way to run a business in a country with no law requiring honest scales at all. She told him plainly that the law had never been the reason she kept hers true.

"A law only tells you what you'll be punished for," she said. "It never tells you what you'll be trusted for. Those are different ledgers, and I've only ever wanted to be rich in the second one."

The first few seasons, this looked—to a young shepherd named Padraig, newly holding his own flock after his father's death the previous winter—like simple foolishness.

Padraig did his sums slowly and carefully at his kitchen table the way his father had taught him, weighing every choice against every other before committing to it. He was twenty-two, scared of failing, scared of dishonoring his father's memory by running the flock into the ground through inexperience or poor judgment. So when the dishonest trader's opening offer came in a hair higher than Bryde's that first year, the difference on paper seemed too plain to argue with.

He sold half his clip to the man. Shook hands on it. Watched the wool weighed out, watched the coins counted onto his table, and felt—briefly—like he'd done well for himself, gotten a fair deal, maybe even a good one.

He only discovered the thumb on the scale later, at home, when he weighed his remaining wool himself on his father's old scale before Bryde's next visit. The numbers didn't match what he'd been paid. Not wildly—not in any way he could have proven to a stranger's satisfaction—but enough that the arithmetic bothered him for days afterward, turning over and over in a mind that had been raised to trust a fair scale as a matter of course.

He didn't confront the trader. The man was gone by then anyway, off in some other valley thumbing some other scale. But the discrepancy sat in Padraig's chest like a stone, the way these things do when you realize you've been taken for slightly more of a fool than you'd like to think of yourself as being.

He did, however, do something else that autumn that he later counted among the more useful decisions of his young life: he asked his aunt—who had kept house for his father in his last years and knew the valley's older traders by reputation—whether she'd ever heard anything said of the dishonest one before he'd arrived.

She had.

She told him, over the kitchen fire one evening when the light was nearly gone and they were both too tired to do much besides talk, of a shepherd two valleys south who had once caught the same trader shorting a fleece by a visible margin and confronted him outright. The trader, she said, had responded smoothly and without apparent shame, saying the scale must have shifted in transport and would be corrected before the next visit.

The correction never came, of course. The trader simply never returned to that particular valley again.

"A man who apologizes for a mistake he has no intention of fixing," his aunt told him, poking at the fire with a stick until it flared, "isn't apologizing. He's buying time to leave."

Padraig turned that piece of advice over for a long while. It colored, more than he perhaps realized at the time, how closely he watched every transaction he made for the rest of his working life. He came to think of it, in later years, as the difference between a mistake and a method. The trader hadn't simply erred once and moved on chastened, which any honest man might do. He had built an entire livelihood on the pattern repeating itself, valley after valley, always leaving before the pattern could be proven against him in any single place.

It was only by comparing notes across several valleys—the way word eventually does travel between shepherds at the larger fairs—that the shape of the whole method became visible at all.

*

Here's what the dishonest trader didn't understand, or understood too late: a valley remembers.

Not loudly. Not in any way that makes for a dramatic confrontation or a satisfying story where the cheat gets publicly shamed and run out of town. Just—quietly, the way information about who can be trusted and who can't be trusted moves through a community that depends on trust to function.

Padraig said nothing to the trader when he returned the following season. But he sold everything to Bryde that year, at her price, without haggling. And when she asked him—mildly surprised, since he'd sold half his clip elsewhere the year before—what had changed his mind, he told her plainly. The whole account. The mismatched numbers. His aunt's story. The pattern he'd started to see.

Bryde listened without interrupting. When he'd finished she only nodded once, as though he'd confirmed something she'd long since stopped needing confirmed, and weighed his fleece.

Padraig was not the only one. A shepherd's wife mentioned the mismatch in her own numbers to a neighbor at the well. The neighbor mentioned it to her husband. The husband, checking his own figures against memory the next time the trader came through, found the same small, deniable shortfall—and said nothing to the trader either. Just sold to Bryde instead the following season, the way Padraig had, without ever needing to make a public accusation of a thing that would have been nearly impossible to prove.

Word travels slow in a valley and then all at once, the way weather does.

Within three seasons the dishonest trader found no one willing to sell to him at all. Not because anyone had ever proven the thumb on his scale in open argument—since none of the individual discrepancies had ever been large enough to argue over on its own—but because a valley remembers, collectively and without needing to discuss it, who has cheated it once.

The trader tried a different valley over the mountain when this one finally closed to him entirely. Word, eventually, traveled there too, carried by shepherds who occasionally crossed the pass to trade at the larger fair on the far side.

He was not seen again in that country.

*

Now here's the part that I think most people miss when they hear this story, or stories like it, because we tend to frame honesty as a moral virtue and dishonesty as a moral failing and leave it at that, which is true as far as it goes but tells you almost nothing about why one trader thrived and the other didn't.

The dishonest trader didn't fail because he was immoral. He failed because he was *expensive*.

Every time he shorted a scale, he was making a trade—a thumb's weight of wool today for the entire valley's business tomorrow. He just didn't realize that was the trade he was making, because the cost didn't come due until later, in a form he hadn't learned to recognize as a cost at all. He thought he was getting away with something. What he was actually doing was systematically destroying the one asset that would have made him wealthy, which was the valley's belief that his scale could be trusted.

Bryde, meanwhile, was making the opposite trade. She was paying—in literal cash, in her own time, in margin she could have kept—for something that didn't show up on any ledger that season. She was buying belief. And belief, it turns out, compounds.

There came a season, some years into Bryde's dealings with the valley, when a hard summer left several households short of coin at exactly the moment their debts to other traders came due. Bryde—under no obligation whatsoever, and at real cost to her own margin that year—extended credit against the following spring's clip to three families who could not have gotten it anywhere else, at fair terms, on nothing more than her own long memory of their honest dealing with her.

One of those families was Padraig's, by then married with children of his own.

He remembered the conversation precisely. Bryde sitting at his kitchen table, going over his own numbers with him line by line, her hands ink-stained from a long day's accounting. When he apologized for having to ask—because a man doesn't like admitting he's short, even to someone he trusts—she told him she wasn't extending him a favor at all.

"I'm collecting on an account you opened the day you decided not to sell to a cheat twice," she said. "You just didn't know you were making a deposit."

Bryde found herself, over the years, with first offer on the best fleeces every season. Shepherds sought her out before the fair even opened. Terms were extended to her that no stranger would have been given—a lamb held back for her at a fair price when supply ran short, a warm bed and a meal on the house when weather caught her on the road, a shepherd's word taken as good enough on a debt of coin she was still owed from a lean season, with no note or witness required.

None of this was charity. It was interest, paid slowly, on a debt of trust she had spent years accumulating one honest weighing at a time. And it compounded, Padraig noticed as he grew older in the trade himself, in exactly the way a well-tended flock compounds—invisibly, for a long while, until suddenly the accumulated advantage was too large to any longer be called small.

"A scale that cheats by a thumb's weight," Bryde told Padraig once, when he asked her outright why she bothered to have hers checked every spring at her own expense, "steals more from the thief than from the shepherd. It costs him a thumb's weight of wool today. It costs him the whole valley tomorrow."

*

I think about this story more than I probably should, especially when I'm tempted to take a shortcut that I know—I *know*—will cost me something later that I can't see clearly yet. Because the thing about belief is that you can't buy it back once you've sold it. You can apologize, you can make restitution, you can promise to do better next time—and sometimes that works, if the breach was small and the history long—but mostly what happens is you just lose the account, and you never quite get it back to where it was.

The dishonest trader thought he was optimizing. He thought he was being smart, getting a little extra margin that nobody would miss, playing the game better than the people who were too naive or too scrupulous to see the angle he'd found.

What he was actually doing was making himself expensive to trust. And in any business where trust is the product—which is every business, eventually, if you're in it long enough—expensive to trust is the same thing as too expensive to do business with.

Bryde wasn't more moral than the other trader. I don't think that's the lesson here, though I know it sounds like it should be. She was just better at math. She'd learned, from her uncle or from experience or from some combination of the two, that the short advantage and the long reputation are rarely for sale at the same price, and the person who chooses the short one always believes, in the moment, that no one is watching closely enough to notice.

Someone is always watching closely enough, eventually. If not this season, then the season the numbers stop matching, quietly, in someone's own accounting at home.

*

Honest weight costs more today and pays more every day after.

That's not a coincidence, or a moral judgment, or a feel-good story about virtue rewarded. It's just the whole of the transaction, laid out plainly. You pay for belief with consistency, with cost borne on your own side, with margin you could have kept but didn't. And what you get back—if you're patient, if you stay in the same place long enough for the valley to remember who you are—is the thing the dishonest trader spent his whole career trying to fake and never managed to buy.

You get to be believed without proving it every time.

Padraig kept his father's old scale in the kitchen for the rest of his working life, and he checked his numbers against everyone else's, every single time, whether or not he trusted them. "The habit costs you nothing when the numbers match," he'd tell younger shepherds who asked him why he bothered. "And it's the only thing that saves you the one time they don't."

But he sold to Bryde, year after year, at her price, without ever asking her to prove the weight again.

That's the trade. That's the whole of it. You either pay for belief on the front end, in margin and cost and inconvenience you'd rather not bear, or you pay for it on the back end, in valleys that stop returning your visits and accounts that close to you one by one until you're working new ground every season, starting from scratch every time, never quite understanding why the business that looked so promising when you started has left you, decades later, no wealthier than when you began.

There is one further detail about Bryde that Maren likes to add when she has the time to tell the fuller version, and I'll tell it here because it's stayed with me longer than almost anything else in this story:

Bryde, in her own old age, sold the trade to a younger woman for less than it was worth on paper—less than another buyer had offered her outright—because the younger woman reminded her of herself at that age, and because Bryde wanted the valley to keep what she'd built there, which wasn't the route or the scale but the *belief* the valley had learned to place in whoever walked through their doors carrying that particular scale.

She could have taken the higher offer. She could have optimized the sale the way the dishonest trader had optimized every transaction he'd ever made.

She didn't. And the valley, which had trusted her for forty years by then, went on trusting the woman who came after her, because Bryde had done the one thing you can't fake and can't buy back once you've sold it:

She'd made being believed worth more to her than the margin she'd have gained by lying.

FIVE — The Lambs Not Yet Born

I was standing in my financial advisor's office when she asked me how many years I thought I had left to work. Not in a morbid way—she just needed a number for the retirement calculator. I said thirty, maybe thirty-five if I stayed healthy. She nodded and started typing.

Then she asked: "And what rate of return are you assuming?"

I gave her the number everyone uses. Seven percent, maybe eight. The historical average. Reasonable.

"And what if it's five?" she asked.

I remember feeling annoyed. Of course it might be five. It might be twelve, too. We can't plan for every possible future, can we? So we pick a reasonable middle and move forward. That's what adults do.

Except—and I should say this up front—I've spent most of my adult life doing exactly that kind of math and then watching it fall apart. Not because I was reckless. Because I kept borrowing against futures I couldn't actually promise would arrive.

Which brings me to Gann.

I met Gann the same week I had that conversation with my advisor, which is probably why his story stuck. He's a sheep farmer in a valley about two hours from where I grew up, and when I say farmer I mean the real kind—the kind who checks on newborn lambs at 3 AM in January and loses sleep over a ewe with mastitis. Not the gentleman-farmer type who hires it all out.

Gann's father had been the same way. Stubborn, proud, the kind of man who would patch a roof with scrap metal rather than ask a neighbor for help. Which is exactly what he did, right up until the winter he died and left Gann with a barn that was more patch than roof.

That first winter after his father passed, Gann stood in that barn during a January storm and watched snow sift through gaps in the tin. The ewes were pregnant—spring lambing season was two months out. The barn needed to be weatherproof by then or he'd lose lambs to the cold, maybe lose ewes too if the stress was bad enough.

He had wool to sell, but not until shearing in April. He had lambs coming, but not until March at the earliest, and they wouldn't be market-weight until summer.

What he had was a roof that wouldn't last another month.

There's a trader who works that valley. Not a shepherd—a money man. He shows up in the fall and sets up in the same spot every year, a tent at the edge of the Saturday market, and he deals in futures. Wool futures, lamb futures, milk futures if you're a dairy man. Cash now for promises later.

Gann had never worked with him before. His father wouldn't have. But his father was dead and the barn was falling apart and the ewes were pregnant and there wasn't time to wait for April.

The trader's terms were straightforward: Gann would promise him thirty lambs in June. In exchange, he'd get the cash now—enough to replace the roof, maybe a bit left over. The price per lamb was fair, maybe even generous. Thirty lambs from a flock of forty-five ewes wasn't greedy. Gann had run the numbers. Even in a bad year he could expect thirty-five, forty lambs easy. Thirty was conservative.

So he signed.

I need to tell you what happened next, but first I should be honest about something: I've done this. Not with sheep—I've never owned a sheep in my life—but I've absolutely borrowed against a future I couldn't guarantee.

In my case it was a business. I was twenty-nine, running a small consulting practice, and I had a client who wanted to sign a year-long contract. Big retainer, steady income, exactly the kind of thing that would let me hire help and stop working seventy-hour weeks. The client was solid. The work was straightforward. It was, by any reasonable assessment, a sure thing.

So I hired two people before the contract was signed.

You can probably guess what happened. The client's board changed priorities. The contract fell through. I had two salaries to pay and no retainer to pay them with.

I'm telling you this because when I describe what Gann did next, I don't want you to think I'm speaking from some place of smug hindsight. I know exactly what it feels like to borrow against a future that seems certain and then watch it dissolve.

Spring came late that year.

Gann's ewes were healthy going into lambing season, but the weather turned. Cold, wet, the kind of March that makes you wonder if winter's ever really going to end. Ewes that should have lambed in early March went late. Some lost their lambs before birth—stress, cold, bad luck. Some lambed twins but could only manage to raise one.

By the time the season was over, Gann had twenty-two live lambs.

Not thirty. Twenty-two.

The trader didn't care. The contract said thirty lambs in June. The trader had already paid. Gann owed thirty lambs or their cash equivalent, and the cash equivalent was more than Gann had.

He sold three of his best ewes to make up the difference.

Not old ewes, not weak ones—the best ones. The ones he'd been planning to breed for years. The foundation of his future flock.

Here's what I remember most from talking to Gann about this: he didn't seem angry. He seemed tired. Like he'd finally understood something he should have known all along.

"The roof needed fixing," he told me. "That's just a fact. But I borrowed against a future I couldn't promise. I treated those lambs like they were already born."

I asked him what he should have done instead.

He thought about it for a while. Then he said: "I should have borrowed against what I had. Against the wool. Against the ewes themselves if I had to. Those were real. The lambs weren't."

You're probably thinking: but that's what loans are. That's how borrowing works. You borrow against future income all the time—mortgages, car loans, student debt. We all do it. That's just modern life.

And you're right. We do.

But there's a difference between borrowing against a future that's reasonably certain and borrowing against one that's just... hoped for.

When you take out a mortgage, you're not borrowing against the possibility of having income. You're borrowing against income you currently have and reasonably expect to continue. If you lose your job, the mortgage doesn't care—but most people don't take out a mortgage while unemployed and hoping to get hired.

What Gann did was closer to taking out a mortgage based on a job interview that went well.

The lambs were always going to be uncertain. Nature doesn't make promises. Ewes get sick, weather turns, things go wrong. Gann knew this—every farmer knows this—but the need was urgent and the future seemed reasonable and he convinced himself that reasonable was the same as guaranteed.

I did the same thing. That client seemed solid. The work was straightforward. By any reasonable assessment, I should have been fine.

But reasonable isn't guaranteed. And when you borrow against reasonable, you're gambling—whether you admit it or not.

Gann's neighbor, an older man named Dubhán, told him something afterward that I think about a lot.

He said: "If you'd needed to borrow, you should have borrowed a share, not a number."

What he meant was this: instead of promising thirty specific lambs, Gann could have offered the trader a percentage of whatever lambs were born. Fifty percent of the spring lambs, say. If it was a great year and he got fifty lambs, the trader would get twenty-five. If it was a terrible year and he only got twenty, the trader would get ten.

The trader would have paid less up front for that deal—of course he would, he'd be taking on more risk. But Gann would have been protected on the downside. A bad lambing season would have cost the trader, not Gann.

Dubhán put it this way: "You can't promise what you don't control. But you can share it."

I think about this every time I'm tempted to make a plan that depends on things going right.

Not going perfectly. Just going right. Going as expected.

Because here's the thing: I'm a planner. I like spreadsheets. I like forecasts. I like knowing what's supposed to happen and when. And there's nothing wrong with that—planning is how you avoid chaos.

But somewhere along the way I started confusing the plan with reality. I started treating the forecast like a promise. Seven percent returns. Thirty lambs. A year-long contract. All reasonable expectations, all well within the realm of normal.

And all subject to conditions I didn't control.

The market might return seven percent on average, but it might return negative fifteen percent next year. The ewes might produce thirty lambs on average, but this year might not be average. The client might have been solid, but their board might change priorities.

Reasonable isn't guaranteed. And when you borrow—whether it's money, time, or commitment—you're making a promise. If you're promising something you don't control, you're gambling.

So what does borrowing wisely actually look like?

First: borrow against what you have, not what you expect to have.

Gann could have borrowed against his wool—he had wool, it was already grown, he just needed to wait until April to sell it. Or he could have borrowed against the ewes themselves, put them up as collateral. Those were real, present assets. The lambs weren't.

In my case, I should have waited until the contract was signed before hiring. Or hired one person instead of two. Or hired contractors instead of employees—people I could scale back if the deal fell through.

I didn't need to avoid risk entirely. I just needed to match my commitments to assets I actually controlled.

Second: if you must borrow against an uncertain future, share the risk.

Dubhán's advice—borrow a share, not a number—is about this. If Gann had offered the trader a percentage instead of a fixed count, they both would have had skin in the game. A bad year would have hurt them both. A great year would have benefited them both.

This shows up in business all the time. Equity instead of salary. Revenue share instead of fixed fees. Commissions instead of retainers. These structures align incentives and share uncertainty.

They pay less when times are good, which is why people avoid them. But they also protect you when times are bad, which is why they're worth considering.

Third—and I think this is the hardest one—stop treating optimization like the goal.

I spent years trying to maximize every variable. Best returns, lowest fees, highest efficiency. And I'm not saying those things don't matter. They do.

But the cost of optimization is often fragility. The more you optimize for everything going right, the more you suffer when things go wrong.

Gann could have kept three extra ewes instead of selling them if he'd borrowed less up front. My business could have survived the lost contract if I'd hired more slowly. Both of us would have been slightly worse off in the good scenario, but dramatically better off in the bad one.

At some point—and I should say I'm still learning this—the goal isn't to win. It's to stop being afraid. To build enough cushion that you can handle a bad lambing season without losing your best ewes. To enjoy the years you have instead of constantly optimizing for the years ahead.

Optimization is the enemy of peace.

When I left Gann's farm that evening, the sun was setting behind the hills and the ewes were grazing in the near pasture. I counted them without thinking—forty-three, including the lambs from that spring. Not a big flock. Probably not an optimized one either, by modern farming standards.

But Gann wasn't afraid of them anymore. Wasn't afraid of a bad winter or a late spring or a trader showing up with a contract. He'd learned what he could promise and what he couldn't, and he'd organized his life around that knowledge.

I thought about my own financial plan. All those projections running out thirty years, built on assumptions about returns and inflation and longevity. Built on lambs not yet born.

What would it look like to build a plan around what I actually had instead?

It would be smaller, probably. Less impressive on a spreadsheet. But it would be mine. And it would sleep better at night.

Here's what you can do Monday morning:

Look at your own commitments. Anything you've borrowed against—mortgage, business loan, personal promise, future expectation. Ask yourself: am I borrowing against what I have, or what I hope to have?

If it's the latter, ask: what happens if the thing I'm hoping for doesn't arrive?

If the answer makes you nervous, that's information. You don't necessarily need to unwind the commitment—but you need to know what you're risking. You need to be honest about whether you're planning or gambling.

And if you're about to make a new commitment—hire someone, sign a contract, promise a specific outcome—ask whether you can structure it as a share instead of a number. A percentage instead of a fixed amount. Something that flexes with reality instead of fighting it.

You'll probably get paid less for that flexibility. But you'll also sleep better when March comes late and cold.

The next chapter is about insurance, which sounds boring until you realize that insurance is just another way of naming the same problem: how do you protect yourself against futures you can't control? But before we get there, I want you to sit with this question for a minute:

What are you counting on that hasn't been born yet?

SIX — The Common Fold

I watched my mother walk past the hay bales at the edge of the common fold one autumn evening, her hand trailing along the rough twine as though checking its weight. She didn't take any. She just stood there, her sons grown and strong beside her, and I saw in her face something I'd only recently learned to recognize: the look of someone who knows they've stayed too long at a table set for emergencies.

The common fold—our valley's shared store of winter feed—was built on a simple premise. When someone's husband dies mid-harvest, or a fire takes half the barn, or lambing season goes catastrophically wrong, you don't make them beg. You don't make them prove they deserve help. You just help. The fold held hay, grain, sometimes tools. More importantly, it held the promise that catastrophe wouldn't mean ruin.

But here's what no one tells you about safety nets: they work so well in crisis that it becomes almost impossible to know when the crisis is over.

My father, Fergal, died when I was fourteen. Pneumonia, sudden and brutal, in the week we should have been cutting hay. My mother, Aveline, had three sons—me the eldest, barely old enough to handle a scythe properly—and a winter coming that we were catastrophically unprepared for. The fold saved us. I mean that literally. We would have lost the farm, probably scattered to different relatives, watching our land get absorbed into someone else's holding while we became hired labor on what used to be ours.

Instead, our neighbors filled the gap. Tadhg brought two cartloads of hay without being asked. Brighid sent her eldest to help with the sheep through lambing. Maren, who kept the fold's tally, marked it all down in her careful hand and never once made my mother feel small for needing it.

That first winter, I felt nothing but gratitude. The second winter, gratitude mixed with determination—I'd work harder, grow stronger, pay it back. The third winter, I felt the first creep of something else. My younger brothers were sixteen and fifteen now, both capable. I was seventeen, doing the work of a grown man. We were still drawing from the fold.

The fourth autumn, Maren came to our gate.

She didn't announce herself with any drama. Just walked up the path at dusk, and I knew from her face that this wasn't a social call. My mother knew too. She wiped her hands on her apron three times before inviting Maren in—a tell I'd learned to read as anxiety.

They sat at our kitchen table, and Maren said, "Aveline, you know I loved Fergal like a brother."

My mother nodded.

"And you know every family in this valley would walk through fire for you and your boys."

Another nod.

"But I need you to understand something." Maren's voice stayed gentle, but there was iron underneath. "The fold is for the fall, not the crawl."

I remember that phrase exactly. *For the fall, not the crawl.* Meaning: when you hit the ground hard, we'll catch you. But once you're back on your feet—even if you're still shaky, still scared, still not sure you're really okay—the net has to drop away. Because if it doesn't, you never learn to walk without it.

You might be thinking this sounds cruel. I thought so too, standing in the doorway listening. My mother had lost her husband. We'd had four years of struggle. Wasn't that enough to earn some grace?

But here's what I understand now that I didn't then: Maren wasn't protecting the hay. She was protecting us.

The fold worked because everyone knew it was temporary. You fell, the community caught you, and then—this was the crucial part—you climbed back up so you could be there when the next person fell. The system only held if people moved through it. If aid hardened into entitlement, the whole structure would collapse. Not today, not this year, but eventually. And when it did, the next family in crisis would find nothing there.

Worse than that, though—and Maren understood this in a way I wouldn't grasp for years—permanent dependence hollows you out from the inside.

My mother had started to change. Small things at first. She'd mention the fold in conversations where it didn't quite fit, as though its existence was the only thing standing between us and disaster. She'd grown cautious about everything, afraid to spend a penny, terrified to make a decision without checking whether we had "enough put by." She'd stopped seeing our farm as something we were building and started seeing it as something we were barely holding onto.

The aid that had saved us was now crippling us.

I've seen this pattern repeat across every kind of help, financial or otherwise. A friend's parents kept paying his rent "just until he got on his feet" for seven years. He's forty now, never quite got on his feet, still calls them when money's tight. Another friend's family gave her a credit card for emergencies in college—she's still using it at thirty-five, and the definition of emergency has expanded to include restaurant meals and vacation flights. The help was real. The need was real, at least at first. But somewhere along the way, the temporary became permanent, and what was supposed to build strength instead built dependency.

Though I should say—and this is important—I did exactly the same thing years later. My daughter got hit with a medical bill she couldn't cover, and I paid it. Fine. Then I paid the next one. And the one after that. And when she asked if I could help with her car payment "just for a couple months," I said yes even though I could see where this was heading. It took my wife pulling me aside and asking, "Are you helping her, or are you making it so she never has to figure this out herself?" before I could admit what I was doing.

So I'm not standing above this looking down. I'm standing in it, looking around.

Back to Maren at our kitchen table. She told my mother that the valley had carried us through the crisis, which was exactly what the fold was for. But my brothers and I were grown now. Capable. And it was time for the accounting to balance.

My mother's face went pale. "I don't have—we can't repay—"

"Not asking for coin," Maren said. "I'm asking for Cormac's time."

She'd worked it out beforehand. Two years of labor, spread across the households that had supported us most. Mending fences for Tadhg. Helping Brighid's family through lambing season. Whatever was needed. Not as hired work—as reciprocity. As the closing of a circle that should never have been left open this long.

I agreed before my mother could object. Partly because I knew Maren was right. Partly because I could feel the weight of those four years pressing down on all of us, and I wanted it gone.

The work itself was harder than I expected. Not physically—I was young and strong. But there's a particular exhaustion that comes from owing. Every morning I woke up aware that I was working off a debt, and every night I went to bed knowing I hadn't cleared it yet. It got into my bones. I started to understand, dimly, what my mother must have been feeling all those years—the constant awareness of being carried by others, the inability to ever quite stand up straight.

I don't think that feeling ever fully leaves you, to be honest. Even now, thirty years later, I sometimes catch myself around the people I worked for during those two years, and some part of me still feels like I owe them something. Which maybe I do. Maybe that's not a bad thing.

But here's what changed: about six months into my labor, I was helping Tadhg replace a section of stone wall that had collapsed, and he said, almost offhand, "Your father did this same stretch twenty years back. Saved my flock that winter."

I hadn't known that.

Tadhg kept working, fitting stones like he was solving a puzzle. "Storm took the wall down, and I was ready to lose half my sheep to the weather. Fergal showed up with your uncles, rebuilt the whole thing in two days. Wouldn't take a penny."

He glanced at me. "This is just the wheel turning, boy. We all fall. We all get lifted. You'll lift someone else someday."

That reframed everything. I'd been thinking of my labor as repayment, which felt like shame. But Tadhg was saying it was just my turn in a rotation that went back generations. My father had lifted him. The valley had lifted us. Now I was lifting them. And someday, when I fell—because everyone falls eventually—someone would lift me.

The wheel keeps turning. That's the only way it works.

By the end of the second year, Maren noted in her tally that our account had balanced. She told me privately, walking back from Brighid's farm one evening. Didn't make an announcement. Didn't need to. The work was done, the debt cleared, and we could move forward as equals again.

My mother changed after that. Not overnight—nothing that deep ever moves fast. But gradually I watched her spine straighten. She started making decisions without hedging. She took a risk on new breeding stock that actually paid off. She laughed more easily. The aid had saved us, absolutely. But clearing the debt freed us.

I think about this now when people talk about financial help between family members, or government assistance programs, or any kind of support structure. The arguments always seem to split into two camps: the people who say aid creates dependency, and the people who say that's heartless and everyone deserves help.

Both are right. Both are also wrong.

Aid creates dependency if it's given without an exit plan, without any expectation that the person receiving it will eventually stand on their own again. But refusing help when someone's genuinely down is just cruelty dressed up as principle. The trick—and it's genuinely difficult—is knowing the difference between *for the fall* and *for the crawl.*

Someone loses their job and needs three months of rent? That's the fall. You help. Same person needs rent covered for the eighteenth month in a row and hasn't seriously looked for work in half that time? That's the crawl. You're not helping anymore; you're enabling.

The problem is that the line between the two isn't always clean, and the person who fell often can't see it themselves. My mother couldn't see it. I couldn't see it with my daughter. It takes someone outside—someone who loves you but isn't drowning with you—to say, "You're standing now. Time to walk."

That's brutal to hear. I know because I've heard it, and I've had to say it, and both are awful.

But here's the cost of not saying it: you trap someone in permanent childhood. You make them fragile. You teach them, deep in their bones, that they're not capable of handling their own life. And that belief becomes self-fulfilling. They'll prove you right by never quite managing to stand on their own, because some part of them has learned that standing isn't necessary. Someone will always catch them.

Until the day no one can.

What happens to the person who's been caught for twenty years when the catcher dies? Or goes broke? Or just gets tired?

I've watched it happen. It's not pretty.

The valley's common fold worked because it operated on a truth that most modern aid systems have forgotten: help is most effective when it's temporary, uncomfortable, and pointed toward independence. The fold didn't make life easy for people who drew from it. My mother had to account for every measure of hay. Maren's tally was public record—everyone knew who was taking and who was giving. There was no shame in needing help, but there was clear expectation that you'd return to giving as soon as you possibly could.

That social pressure—not harsh, but real—kept the system healthy.

When we remove that pressure entirely, when we make aid so comfortable that there's no real reason to climb back up, we think we're being compassionate. We're actually being cruel. We're trading someone's short-term comfort for their long-term dignity.

Though I should say, I still err on the side of giving too much rather than too little. I can't help it. When someone I love is struggling, every instinct in me wants to fix it for them. I've bailed out my kids more times than I should have. I've lent money to friends I knew wouldn't pay it back. I'm not good at drawing the line.

But I know where the line is now, even if I can't always hold it. That's something.

Maren died ten years ago. At her funeral, person after person stood up and told some version of the same story: she'd helped them when they'd fallen, then refused to let them stay down. She'd been strict about it, almost cold sometimes. But every single person credited her with saving not just their circumstances but their self-respect.

The fold itself doesn't exist anymore—the valley modernized, things changed, the old systems fell away. But I still think about it whenever I'm faced with the question of how to help someone without hurting them.

And I'm still not sure I've figured it out.

What I do know is this: the most generous thing you can do for someone who's fallen is catch them, then make sure they remember how to walk. Catching them is the easy part. Love does that automatically. The hard part—the part that actually requires discipline and wisdom and genuine care—is knowing when to let go.

My mother lived another twenty years after Maren came to our gate that evening. In those years, she helped three other families through their own crises, gave labor and resources freely, became someone others leaned on. None of that would have happened if Maren hadn't forced us to balance the account.

The aid saved us. But clearing the debt made us whole.

You're probably wondering what this means for you, specifically. Whether you're the one giving help that's gone on too long, or receiving it. Whether you should cut someone off, or keep supporting them, or ask for help yourself but you're afraid it'll trap you the way I've described.

I don't have a clean answer. I told you I'm not good at holding the line myself.

But I know the question you should be asking: Is this help building strength or replacing it?

If you're giving aid and the person receiving it is gradually getting stronger, more capable, more independent—even if it's slow, even if there are setbacks—you're probably doing it right. Keep going.

If you're giving aid and the person is getting more fragile, more dependent, less able to imagine handling their own life, you're probably doing harm. No matter how much love is behind it.

And if you're the one receiving help, ask yourself: Am I walking yet? Could I be, if I had to? Or have I settled into being carried?

That last question is the hardest one to answer honestly.

SEVEN — The One Valley

Every generation or two, the valley produces a family whose good fortune becomes, without anyone intending it, a kind of quiet lesson to everyone watching — not because the family did anything wrong in the years their fortune was rising, but because good ground and good breeding can make a family forget that fortune is never simply owned outright. It is only ever held, for as long as circumstance allows, and circumstance owes no household an explanation before it changes its mind. The Dunmores learned this the hard way, in a single season, after three generations of not needing to learn it at all.

There was a flock, three generations built, that grazed only ever in a single sheltered valley — good grass, a gentle stream, walls kept in careful repair, a pasture so well-suited to sheep that the family who owned it, the Dunmores, had never once in living memory thought to graze anywhere else. Why would they. The valley gave them everything a flock could want, tucked as it was between two shoulders of hill that broke the worst of the winter wind, watered by a stream that never ran dry even in the driest summers other farms complained of, grassed thick and green from the same rich, low-lying soil that made it, in every ordinary sense, the envy of every shepherd who had ever walked its boundary and wished, quietly, that their own inheritance had been half so kind.

The valley's other shepherds had, over three generations, developed a kind of running fondness for the Dunmore land that was not quite envy and not quite admiration but something adjacent to both — the way any community feels about the one household whose good fortune seems, on the surface, entirely uncomplicated. Young shepherds newly given their first flock would sometimes be told, half in jest, that they should hope for ground half so kind as the Dunmores' before they ever hoped for skill, since skill, the old joke went, could be taught, but ground like that only ever came from an ancestor's good luck.

It was Bevan Dunmore's grandfather who first cleared it, his father who walled it, and Bevan himself who inherited it at the height of its productivity — the richest grass, the best-bred flock the valley had seen, numbers that made every neighboring shepherd's holdings look modest by comparison. Bevan had grown up being told, by his father and by every visitor who ever walked the boundary wall with him, that he had inherited the finest piece of grazing land in the whole country, and he had never once had cause to doubt it. Why would he divide his attention, and his flock's grazing, across lesser ground when the ground he already had gave him everything a shepherd could reasonably want.

A sickness came through that valley the summer Bevan turned thirty — a foot-rot that spreads through wet, sheltered ground exactly like the kind that had always made his pasture so good for grazing in the first place, the same shelter and the same gentle stream that had been the valley's whole blessing becoming, in a single season, the very conditions the sickness needed to spread through every animal that shared it. It began, as it usually does, quietly — a limping ewe here, a swollen hoof there, nothing that alarmed him at first, since a limping animal is an ordinary enough sight in any flock of size. By the time he understood what he was looking at, walking his own pasture one grey morning and counting a dozen animals favoring a foot, the sickness had already had the better part of three weeks to move through ground where every animal drank from the same stream and sheltered, night after night, in the same handful of low, wind-broken hollows. Because the entire flock grazed the same ground, drank the same stream, sheltered under the same lee of hill, the sickness that found one animal found nearly all of them within the month.

Ossla's own mother had come from a country further south, married into this valley as a young woman, and had brought with her, along with her dowry flock, a habit of mind that had never fully taken root among the families who'd farmed this particular valley for generations — a habit of assuming, quietly and without needing dramatic proof, that any single piece of good fortune could turn on you, and that the wise response was never to refuse the good fortune but simply never to depend on it entirely. She had taught this to Ossla the way most such lessons pass between mothers and daughters, less through direct instruction than through the simple, repeated example of decisions made a certain way, year after year, without much explanation offered or needed. Two valleys over, a shepherd named Ossla — no relation to old Ossian, though the names are close enough that Maren always pauses to say so — had built her flock differently, without ever being able to say exactly why she'd done it that way except that her mother had taught her to. Ossla grazed a third of her flock in the low home pasture, a third in a higher meadow a half-day's walk distant, and a third further still, on land she leased from a neighboring family entirely, ground that shared no stream, no shelter, no soil with the other two.

Neighboring shepherds who watched Ossla divide her time and labor across three pastures each season sometimes remarked, not unkindly, that she seemed to be making her own work harder than it needed to be, and a few of the more direct among them said as much to her face over the years, wondering aloud why a woman with grazing rights to such good home pasture didn't simply concentrate her flock the way any sensible shepherd would. She took the comments in good humor, mostly, and rarely argued the point at length, since the whole logic of what she was doing was difficult to defend convincingly against a hazard that had not yet happened and might, for all anyone standing in an ordinary summer could tell, never happen at all. It was, by every measure Bevan would have applied, a less efficient way to keep sheep. Ossla spent half her season walking between three pastures instead of tending one. Her flock never grew as large, in any single year, as a flock that could pour every hour of care into a single perfect valley.

But when the foot-rot came through that summer — and it came through Ossla's home pasture too, sparing no one entirely — it found only a third of her flock to spread through, because the other two-thirds grazed ground the sickness had never touched. She lost animals. She did not lose the flock.

The valley's tally-keeper that year, Maren's own predecessor, recorded the loss in the plainest possible terms in the yearly ledger, a single stark line noting the largest single-season decline in flock numbers the valley had seen in living memory, and it is that entry, more than any of the family's own private grief, that Maren points to whenever she wants to show a skeptical listener that this story is not merely embellishment added in the retelling. Bevan lost, by the time the sickness had run its course, better than half of three generations' careful breeding, all of it gone within a single season because all of it had, without his ever quite deciding so on purpose, been standing in the same place at the same time. He spent that autumn walking a pasture with barely half the animals it had carried in spring, the grass — ironically, cruelly — richer and more plentiful than it had been in years, with far fewer mouths left to graze it, a kind of abundance that felt, he said afterward, like the valley mocking him for a mistake it had spent three generations letting him believe was simply good fortune.

In the months between the sickness running its course and that winter visit, Bevan had done what most men do after a catastrophe they didn't see coming: he had turned the disaster over and over in his mind searching for the moment he could have prevented it, and had come up, again and again, empty. There had been no single bad decision he could point to — no reckless purchase, no ignored warning, no obvious carelessness in the flock's daily care. The sickness itself was simply bad luck, the kind that visits every valley eventually. What haunted him was not the bad luck. It was the discovery that a lifetime of otherwise excellent shepherding had left his family with no defense against it whatsoever, because the very thing that made his pasture so consistently excellent — its unity, its concentration, everything poured into one perfect piece of ground — was the same thing that had let one piece of bad luck become total.

He rode over, that winter, to the valley where Ossla kept her divided flock, having heard by then how lightly the same sickness had touched her, and asked her plainly how she'd known to spread her animals across three separate pastures when nothing in the valley's ordinary wisdom suggested such a thing was necessary. She told him, honestly, that she hadn't known — not the way he meant it, not as a deliberate answer to a risk she could have named in advance. "My mother simply never trusted one piece of ground with everything," she said. "She couldn't have told you why either, if you'd asked her outright. She only knew that a single bad season shouldn't be able to end a family, and dividing the flock was the only way she knew to make that true without knowing which particular bad season it might turn out to be."

The second pasture Bevan leased, once he'd found ground he judged suitably distant and suitably different in its soil and drainage from his home valley, took him the better part of two years to properly establish — new fencing, new water arrangements with the family who owned the adjoining land, a season spent simply learning its hazards the slow way every shepherd eventually must learn any unfamiliar ground. He rebuilt, in the years after, the way his grandfather had first built — but this time with a second, smaller pasture leased a half-day's walk from the first, a decision that cost him convenience every season for the rest of his life, extra walking, extra fencing, a flock that never again grew quite as fast in any single good year as it might have grown concentrated on his one rich valley alone — and that he never once, watching Ossla's flock weather two more sicknesses over the following decade that his own single valley would not have survived, regretted making.

The valley that gives everything a flock could want is also the valley that can take everything away in a single season, if the flock never learns to stand anywhere else. What looks like inefficiency — the walking, the divided attention, the smaller yearly growth — is very often just risk, paid down in advance, in a currency you don't notice you're spending until the season it saves you.

The common fold still stands at the low end of our valley, tended in rotation the same way it has been for longer than anyone can properly account for, and the reckoning still happens each autumn with cider passed around while the tallies are read aloud. I have sat at that reckoning more autumns than I can easily count now, and I have watched, more than once, a family's private arithmetic quietly go the way Aveline's did — not from any real unkindness in them, but from the simple, human difficulty of noticing, from the inside, exactly when a rescue has finished its work and settled into something else.

EIGHT — The Wall Between Winters

I've told you Fintan checked his walls twice a year, every year, without fail. That's the advice I should give you—set a calendar reminder, make it automatic, treat it like a non-negotiable appointment with your future self.

Though I should say: I didn't do that for the first eight years I owned property.

What I did instead was notice a loose stone, think "I should fix that," walk past it for six months, notice it again, think "definitely this weekend," and then one February morning discover that the entire section had collapsed in a storm I'd barely noticed from inside my warm house. No sheep died in my case—I don't keep sheep, despite what this book might suggest—but I did spend £1,400 on emergency repairs that would have cost me maybe forty quid and an afternoon if I'd just... not been an idiot about it.

Fintan wasn't an idiot about it.

The thing about Fintan—and I learned this from his grandson, who still farms the same land—is that he didn't check his walls because he was particularly virtuous or disciplined. He checked them because he was, to be honest, a bit paranoid. His father had lost sheep to a wall breach when Fintan was seven years old, and the image of his father standing in the snow, counting the missing ewes, looking suddenly old in a way that terrified young Fintan—that image never left him.

Fear can be useful. Not the chronic anxiety that keeps you awake at three in the morning, but the clean, specific fear that says: I know exactly what happens if I don't do this thing, and I refuse to let it happen.

Declan had no such image in his head.

Declan's father had been lucky, or maybe just more diligent than Declan himself, and Declan had never personally witnessed the cost of a failed wall. He'd heard the stories, certainly. Every shepherd in the valley knew someone who knew someone who'd lost stock to a breach. But knowing intellectually that something can happen is different—physiologically different, neurologically different—from having seen it.

So each autumn, when the light turned golden and the first frosts began to silver the grass, Declan would walk his portion of the wall. He'd notice things. A stone shifted slightly out of true. A section where the mortar (such as it was—these were dry stone walls, mostly, but some sections had been patched with cement over the years) had cracked and fallen away. Ivy pushing between the stones, which seems decorative until you understand that ivy roots can, over the course of a winter's freeze-thaw cycle, wedge stones apart as effectively as a crowbar.

He'd notice these things. He'd think: I should deal with that.

And then the day would get away from him.

I want to be clear about something, because I think this matters for understanding how this kind of failure happens: Declan wasn't lazy. The man ran a tight operation. His lambing percentage was consistently among the best in the valley. His fleece quality was exceptional. He was, by any reasonable standard, a successful shepherd.

But he'd developed a kind of... optimistic accounting when it came to the wall.

Each year he'd walk it, see the problems, estimate maybe four hours of work needed, and then tell himself he'd get to it "before the weather turns." The problem was that "before the weather turns" is not actually a date. It's a floating deadline that recedes as you approach it. The weather is always about to turn. That's what weather does.

And then winter would arrive—gradually at first, then suddenly—and by the time the real cold set in, working on a wall meant frozen fingers and stones too cold to handle comfortably, and he'd think: Well, it held last winter. Probably fine for one more season. I'll definitely deal with it in spring.

Spring, of course, brought lambing. Then shearing. Then summer grazing management. Then autumn, and the cycle would begin again, each year's neglect compounding quietly, invisibly, until the wall wasn't just neglected—it was structurally compromised in ways that weren't obvious to a casual glance but were absolutely obvious to the wind.

The storm that finally brought down Declan's wall wasn't even particularly remarkable.

January, yes, so proper winter, but not the worst storm that season. Fintan's wall—forty meters away, built from the same stone by the same hands a century earlier—stood firm. Didn't lose a single stone. Because Fintan had, the previous October, spent an afternoon resetting the section that had looked slightly off.

Declan woke on the morning of January 17th—I know the date because it's recorded in the local paper; unusual sheep deaths get noted in rural valleys—to find his wall breached. Not collapsed entirely. Just a gap, maybe two meters wide, where the compromised section had finally given way.

And fourteen ewes, heavy with lamb, had pushed through that gap during the night, looking for shelter from the wind, and had ended up in a steep-sided gully they couldn't climb out of. The temperature that night had dropped to minus eight.

When Declan found them at first light, some were already dead. Others were in the process of dying. He did what he could—got five of them out alive, though one of those five later lost her lamb. The rest he had to watch die, or end their suffering himself when it was clear they wouldn't recover.

I'm dwelling on this—I know I am—because I need you to feel it. Not just know it intellectually, but feel it. The specific texture of that morning. Declan standing in the frost, breath clouding, looking at animals he'd raised from birth, animals whose mothers and grandmothers he'd known, animals he'd planned to see through lambing in another month—looking at them dead or dying because he hadn't spent four hours fixing a wall.

His son helped him that morning. Cian was sixteen, old enough to understand exactly what he was witnessing. Old enough to do the math on what fourteen ewes represented in lost income. Old enough to see his father's face and understand that the financial loss, substantial as it was, wasn't actually the worst part.

The worst part was that it had been preventable.

Not "preventable if Declan had been more lucky" or "preventable if he'd had information he didn't have." Preventable if he'd done the thing he knew he needed to do and had actively chosen not to do fourteen separate times over seven years.

That evening—and Cian told me this story himself, years later, when I was researching this book—Cian asked his father a question that probably every child eventually asks a parent who's made a visible, costly mistake: "Why didn't you just fix it?"

Declan's answer is worth recording exactly as Cian remembered it: "Because it never felt urgent enough to be worth the bother until it was too late for fixing to matter."

There's a specific kind of financial mistake that follows this exact pattern, and if you're reading this book, you've almost certainly made it. Maybe not the wall version. Maybe the "I should really look at my pension" version, or the "I should set up that emergency fund" version, or the "I should deal with that small debt before it compounds" version.

The thing these mistakes have in common is that they're:

1. Easy to fix early 2. Expensive or impossible to fix late 3. Never urgent until the moment they become catastrophic 4. Obvious in retrospect

You know what you're supposed to do about these things. You've known for years. You could probably lecture someone else about the importance of doing them. But you haven't done them, because doing them requires you to carve time out of a day that already feels too full to address a problem that isn't yet painful.

This is the wall between winters.

Not the wall that protects you through one specific winter, but the wall that stands between your current season and all your future seasons. The maintenance you do—or don't do—in the ordinary time determines what happens when the extraordinary time arrives.

Fintan and Declan rebuilt the breached section together that week. Took them three days of hard work. Fintan didn't lord it over Declan—didn't say "I told you so" or make pointed comments about diligence. Just showed up and worked. That's what neighbors do in a valley where everyone understands that pride is less important than survival.

But the work of rebuilding was different from the work of maintaining, and both men knew it. Heavier. Colder, because they were doing it in January instead of October. More expensive, because they had to hire a truck to bring in replacement stones—some of the original stones had shattered in the fall. And haunted by the knowledge of what the delay had cost.

Declan changed after that winter. Cian said his father became almost obsessive about maintenance—not just walls, but everything. Checked fences weekly. Serviced equipment early. Replaced worn parts before they failed. It was as if the wall breach had flipped some switch in his brain, moved maintenance from the category of "things I should do when I get around to it" to "things that are actually urgent whether they feel urgent or not."

But here's what interests me: Declan's transformation, though genuine, came at the cost of fourteen ewes and all their unborn lambs. Call it roughly £3,000 in direct losses, plus the ongoing lost production from those bloodlines. Expensive education.

Fintan's education had been cheaper—just the childhood memory of his father's face in the snow, which cost him nothing but gave him the same knowledge.

If you can learn from observation rather than experience, you get the knowledge without paying the tuition. That's why I'm telling you this story instead of waiting for you to live it.

So here's what I want you to do—not someday, not when you get around to it, but Monday:

Pick one specific financial boundary that you know needs maintenance but that you've been avoiding because it's not yet urgent. Your emergency fund that's been sitting at £400 for two years. The pension contribution you keep meaning to increase. The insurance coverage you've been meaning to review. The debt repayment plan you've been meaning to start.

Not all of them. One. The one that, if you're honest with yourself, you're most afraid might fail spectacularly if you don't address it.

Put four hours in your calendar for this month. Actual blocked time, not "I'll find time somehow." Four hours is what Declan needed. It's probably what you need.

And then do the thing.

Not because you're particularly virtuous or disciplined, but because you've now seen—through Declan's eyes, through mine—what it looks like when you don't. You have the image in your head. The wall breached, the stock lost, the preventable disaster that you prevented by the simple act of not being an idiot about maintenance.

Will four hours this month prevent every possible disaster? Of course not. Some storms bring down even well-maintained walls. Some financial catastrophes arrive regardless of how carefully you've prepared.

But most don't.

Most of the walls that fail do so because someone walked past them for seven years thinking "I should fix that" and never quite getting around to it.

Don't be Declan. At least not about this.

Though I should mention—because I'd be lying if I presented myself as someone who learned this lesson once and never struggled with it again—I still have areas of my financial life where I'm absolutely being Declan right now. Things I know I should address and haven't. The difference is that now I know I'm doing it, which means I'm making an active choice rather than just drifting into neglect.

Sometimes that choice is even defensible. If you've got three walls that need work and only time to maintain one, you're going to have to let something slide. The skill is in choosing which wall you can afford to let deteriorate and which one you absolutely can't.

But you have to choose. You can't just pretend you're maintaining all three when you're maintaining none.

Cian still farms his father's land. He checks his walls in early October and again in March, every year, without fail. His children do the same. Declan's grandson, who never met the ewes that died before he was born, still hears the story every autumn when wall-checking time comes around.

Some lessons echo longer than the stones that taught them.

NINE — The Shepherd's Name

The thank-you card is still on my desk. Cream cardstock, the kind you buy at Hallmark when you want to say something important. She signed it "With gratitude, Ellen" and included a P.S.: "Looking forward to our retirement plans coming together!"

I received it in October 2006, three days after we closed on her second rental property.

Ellen was a middle school science teacher. Fifty-nine years old. Three years from retirement. She'd saved $127,000 over thirty years of teaching—not through any sophisticated strategy, just automatic deposits from every paycheck into a savings account that paid 2.3% interest. When she first sat across from me in my office, she asked one question: "Is this enough?"

I told her it wasn't. Real estate, I explained, was *different this time*. The fundamentals had changed. We were in a new paradigm. I used those exact words—"new paradigm"—without a trace of irony, and she wrote them down in her notebook like I was delivering prophecy instead of recycling the same garbage everyone at my firm was saying at happy hour.

She put 40% of her savings into a down payment.

Eighteen months later, the property was worth less than she owed on it. The renters stopped paying. The bank sent letters. Ellen postponed her retirement by four years, picked up summer school teaching, and never mentioned my name to anyone. Not to complain. Not to warn others. She just went quiet.

I know this because I called her. Twice. She was polite both times. Said it wasn't my fault, that she'd made her own decision.

Which was true and also completely irrelevant, because we both knew I'd been the one holding the pen when she signed.

The card sits next to my coffee cup. I look at it most mornings. Not because I'm flagellating myself—I did that for the first year—but because it's the cheapest tuition I've ever paid for the most expensive lesson: your name is the only asset that compounds in both directions.

Here's what I mean.

In 1991, Salomon Brothers—one of Wall Street's most prestigious firms—got caught rigging Treasury bond auctions. The details don't matter. What matters is what Warren Buffett did next. He was the largest shareholder. He could have stayed in Omaha, released a statement through lawyers, protected his capital. Instead, he moved to New York, took over as interim chairman, and spent nine hours testifying before Congress. His opening line: "Lose money for the firm, and I will be understanding. Lose a shred of reputation for the firm, and I will be ruthless."

Salomon survived. Buffett's reputation—already strong—became something else entirely. That testimony is still taught in business schools, not because of what he said about bonds but because of what he demonstrated about names.

Now consider the opposite.

Bernie Madoff ran the largest Ponzi scheme in history for seventeen years. Sixty-five billion dollars. Thousands of victims. But here's the part that keeps me up: he didn't do it by being unknown. He did it by being *trusted.* He was the former chairman of NASDAQ. He sat on nonprofit boards. He had a reputation—an expensive, carefully maintained, utterly counterfeit reputation—and he traded on it until there was nothing left to trade.

When he was finally arrested in 2008, his sons turned him in. His own children couldn't live with the name he'd built.

One man protected a name that wasn't even his own firm's. Another destroyed a name that bore his family's legacy. The difference wasn't intelligence or capital or market conditions. It was intention. Buffett understood that reputation is the asset; everything else is just inventory. Madoff understood that reputation is camouflage; the asset is the con.

Most of us live somewhere between those extremes. We're not billionaires or criminals. We're just trying to pay the mortgage and maybe, if we're lucky, leave something behind besides debt. But the principle scales. Your name—what people think when they hear it, what they tell others when you're not in the room—is either appreciating or depreciating. There's no neutral.

Ellen's card taught me that. Not on the day I received it, but four years later, when I ran into her at a Starbucks near the school where she taught. She was grading lab reports. I almost walked past, but she looked up and smiled—genuinely—and waved me over.

"How've you been?" she asked.

I told her fine. Asked how retirement planning was going. She said she'd simplified things, just putting everything back into savings, wasn't trying to get fancy anymore. Then she asked if I wanted to sit down.

I did, though I should say—I almost didn't. Part of me wanted to nod politely and leave, avoid the whole conversation. But I sat, and we talked for twenty minutes about nothing important, and at the end she said, "You know, I never blamed you. You were doing your job."

I'd never blamed her for not blaming me. That wasn't the problem. The problem was that I'd spent four years rebuilding my own standards for what "my job" meant, and her forgiveness—unasked for, freely given—felt less like absolution and more like an audit I hadn't studied for.

That night, I made a list. Not a goals list or a vision board. A list of every client I'd advised in the previous five years. Next to each name, I wrote one question: *If they lost everything tomorrow, would they tell others to trust me?*

Twelve names out of forty-three got a checkmark.

Twelve.

I'd spent half a decade building a book of business and apparently torched my actual reputation with 72% of the people I'd served. Some of that was market timing—2008 was brutal for everyone. Some was bad luck. But most of it, if I'm honest, was me giving advice that sounded good in the moment and looked good on a commission statement but didn't actually account for what would happen if I was wrong.

Which I was. Often.

So what do you actually *do* with this? Because the worst kind of self-help chapter is the one that makes you feel bad about your past and then offers nothing except a vague exhortation to "be better." I've read those chapters. I've *written* those chapters. They're garbage.

Here's what I did, and what I'd recommend you do, though I should say—what I'd recommend and what I actually did are different things, because I'm a human and not a motivational poster.

First: Write down the names.

Not metaphorically. Literally. Get a notebook—a physical one, not a Notes app—and write down the names of people whose opinion of you matters. Not everyone. Not your fourth-grade teacher or the barista who misspells your name. The people whose trust you've asked for, explicitly or implicitly. Your clients, if you have them. Your boss. Your direct reports. Your spouse. Your kids, if they're old enough to have opinions about your character.

Then ask the uncomfortable question: *If they were describing me to someone who'd never met me, what would they say?*

Not what you hope they'd say. What they'd *actually* say, based on your recent actions.

I did this exercise in 2010. Came up with nineteen names. Wrote down what I thought each would say. Then—and this is the part that requires either courage or stupidity, I'm still not sure which—I called six of them and asked directly.

Two people were kinder than I expected. Four were blunter. One guy, a former client who'd moved his accounts elsewhere, said, "Honestly? I'd say you're smart but you care more about looking right than being right."

That one got added to the card on my desk. Imaginary card. I didn't actually write it down. But it landed the same way.

Second: Pick one name and repair it.

You can't fix nineteen relationships in a week. You can't even fix nineteen relationships in a year. But you can fix one. Maybe two, if they're small repairs.

I started with a guy named Tom. He'd been a client in 2007, pulled his money after the crash, never returned my calls. I tracked down his new email—he'd changed firms—and sent him a message. Three sentences: *I gave you bad advice in 2007. It cost you money and I didn't own it at the time. I'm sorry.*

He wrote back two days later. Said he appreciated it, but he'd moved on. Didn't want to rehash it. That was fine. The apology wasn't a negotiation. It wasn't me trying to win him back. It was me cleaning up something I'd left broken.

Did it change his opinion of me? Maybe, maybe not. But it changed my opinion of me, and that turned out to matter more than I expected.

Third: Stop doing the thing that's eroding your name.

This one's harder because it requires diagnosing the pattern, and most of us are exceptionally skilled at lying to ourselves about our patterns.

For me, the pattern was saying yes when I should've said "I don't know." A client would ask about an investment, and instead of admitting uncertainty, I'd construct a confident-sounding answer from half-remembered research and optimistic assumptions. It felt like helping. It wasn't helping. It was performing competence at the expense of honesty.

So I started saying "I don't know" out loud. In meetings. On calls. In emails. Just the phrase, clean and complete: *I don't know.*

The first three times I said it, I felt like I was admitting malpractice. By the tenth time, I realized it was the most valuable thing I could say. Clients didn't need me to know everything. They needed me to know what I knew and admit what I didn't.

That shift—from performance to transparency—did more for my reputation in eighteen months than the previous decade of trying to sound smart.

Fourth: Track the deposits.

Reputation isn't built in grand gestures. It's built in tiny, forgettable moments that compound over time. Returning a call when you said you would. Admitting a mistake before someone else finds it. Keeping a confidence. Giving credit. Underpromising and overdelivering, not because it's strategic but because it's sustainable.

I started keeping a second list—just a running tally of moments where I had a choice between the easy thing and the right thing, and I picked the right thing. Not to congratulate myself. To notice the pattern. Because what you track, you improve, and what you improve becomes who you are.

Some weeks the list was long. Some weeks it was empty. But over time, the baseline shifted. The default choice became the one that built instead of borrowed.

There's a story I think about sometimes, though I can't verify all the details so take it as illustrative rather than factual. Ray Kroc, the man who turned McDonald's into a global empire, supposedly once fired a franchise operator who was running a profitable location. The operator had cut corners—used cheaper beef, skimped on cleaning, pocketed the difference. The franchise was making money. Customers hadn't noticed yet. But Kroc showed up unannounced, saw what was happening, and revoked the license on the spot.

The operator protested. Said he was meeting sales targets. Kroc's response, according to the version I heard: "You're not selling hamburgers. You're selling McDonald's. And you just made the name worth less."

I don't know if that exact conversation happened. But I know the principle is sound. Every transaction you make is either adding to or withdrawing from the accumulated trust attached to your name. You can get away with withdrawals for a while—longer than you'd think—but eventually, the account goes negative, and no amount of charm or competence will bring it back.

Ellen forgave me. Tom acknowledged my apology. But neither of them trusted me with their money again, and they were right not to. I'd made a withdrawal I couldn't repay in kind. The best I could do was stop making new ones.

You might be wondering—and this is the question I get when I tell this story to younger advisors—whether this is all just naive idealism. Whether the world actually rewards integrity or just pretends to while promoting the people who cut corners more elegantly.

Fair question. And the answer is: both.

Yes, some people cheat and win. Yes, some liars retire rich and die comfortable. The world is not a morality play. But here's the thing I've noticed over twenty years in this industry: the people who build

reputations instead of brands sleep better. They don't check their phones at 2 a.m. wondering who's about to discover what. They don't spend energy maintaining false versions of themselves. And when things go wrong—because they always do, eventually—they have reserves of trust to draw on that no amount of money can buy after the fact.

That's not karma. It's compounding. The same principle that makes your retirement account grow makes your reputation grow, except reputation compounds faster and crashes harder.

So no, I'm not telling you that good guys always finish first. I'm telling you that finishing first isn't the point. The point is being able to finish at all, and still recognize yourself when you cross the line.

Here's what I want you to do Monday morning.

Not "think about." Not "consider exploring." Actually do.

Open your email. Find the last message where you said you'd follow up and didn't. Reply to it. Two sentences: acknowledge the gap, complete the follow-up. Don't explain why it took so long. Just close the loop.

Then find one person you've borrowed trust from—a promise you didn't keep, a standard you didn't meet, a expectation you missed—and send them the same three sentences I sent Tom. *I said X. I did Y. I'm sorry.*

That's it. No grand campaign. No twelve-step reputation-building seminar. Just two small deposits in accounts that have been overdrafted.

You'll be surprised how much those two actions compound.

And if you do nothing else from this chapter—if every other word evaporates from memory—remember this: Ellen still sent me a Christmas card every year until she retired in 2014. Not because I'd made her rich. Because I'd called her after I'd cost her money, and I'd kept calling, and eventually she concluded that I cared more about her than I did about hiding.

She was right. It just took me longer than it should have to prove it.

The name you build isn't the one you put on your business card. It's the one other people use when you're not in the room. And the only way to control that name is to stop trying to control it and start earning it, one forgettable decision at a time.

That's the work. Not glamorous. Not fast. But it's the work that lasts longer than your portfolio, your job title, or the balance in your retirement account.

Your name is what remains when everything else burns down.

Make sure it's fireproof.

TEN — The Far Green

I watched my last consulting client walk out of the coffee shop on a Tuesday afternoon in November, three years after I should have closed the practice. He was a nice enough guy—ran a small logistics company, always paid on time—but I'd spent the previous forty-five minutes explaining the same inventory management principles I'd explained to him four times before. He nodded, thanked me, said he'd implement it this time. I knew he wouldn't. And I knew I'd keep billing him anyway, because I'd convinced myself that walking away from this business meant admitting I'd wasted the previous five years building it.

That's the thing about greener grass. By the time you realize you've been standing on it for three years and it's turned to mud under your feet, you've usually burned through whatever cushion you had to retreat to solid ground.

The financial advice industry loves to talk about opportunity cost—what you give up when you choose one investment over another. But nobody talks about the stickiness cost, the price you pay for refusing to admit that the "next big thing" you chased turned out to be a dead end. I kept that consulting practice alive long past its expiration date, not because it was profitable (it barely covered its own overhead by the end), but because closing it would mean looking at those five years of effort and calling them what they were: a detour I could have exited three years earlier.

Though I should say—and this is the uncomfortable truth I wish someone had told me back then—the real cost wasn't the money I burned through. It was the three years I spent defending a decision I'd already stopped believing in.

The Bible gives us Osric on his ridge, staring at distant pastures that shimmer with promise. Every shepherd knows that view. The grass always looks thicker from a distance, the slopes gentler, the water clearer. What the parable doesn't tell you—though I suspect the shepherds reading it understood—is what happens when you actually walk to that far green and discover it's just grass. Different grass, maybe. Grass with its own problems, its own thin patches and rocky soil. But not the paradise you imagined from half a mile away.

Here's what makes this trap so vicious: the moment you arrive at the "greener" pasture, you can see another ridge in the distance, and *that* grass looks even better. The game never ends. You can spend your entire life chasing the shimmer on the horizon and never once stop to ask whether the pasture under your feet might be worth improving.

I'm not talking about ambition. Ambition is seeing potential and building toward it. I'm talking about the chronic restlessness that mistake for vision—the inability to commit to optimizing what you have because you're always half-convinced that the real opportunity is somewhere else.

Let me give you a pattern you can verify yourself, because I can't cite you a study but I can tell you what to look for: watch people who change jobs every eighteen months to two years, always chasing a better title or a higher salary. (Not people who leave bad situations—I mean people who leave *fine* situations for *slightly better* situations.) Track them for a decade. You'll notice something. They're not climbing. They're churning. Each move looks like progress in isolation, but the pattern adds up to nowhere, because they're never in one place long enough to compound their gains. They're always the new person, always proving themselves, always starting over.

The wealth equivalent is the investor who can't stick with an index fund for ten years because they keep hearing about some new strategy. Real estate! No wait, crypto! No wait, dividend stocks! They're not wrong that each of these can build wealth. They're wrong to assume that switching between them is better than mastering one.

You might be thinking, "But what if I really *am* in the wrong pasture? What if my job is genuinely bad, or my business model is broken, or I'm in the wrong field entirely?" Fair question. I've asked it myself, usually around two in the morning when I couldn't sleep because I was trying to decide whether to shut down the consulting practice or double down on it.

Here's the uncomfortable test I eventually developed, though to be honest I didn't apply it until it was too late: If you removed the fear of admitting you were wrong, would you still want to stay?

That's it. That's the whole diagnostic.

If the only reason you're holding onto something—a business, a job, an investment strategy—is because walking away would mean admitting the past five years (or ten, or twenty) were a mistake, you're not evaluating the opportunity. You're defending your ego. And ego is the most expensive overhead you can carry.

When I finally closed the consulting practice, I had to call each client and explain I was shutting down. I expected it to feel like failure. Instead, it felt like waking up from a dream I'd been trying to force myself to keep dreaming. One of the clients—a woman who ran a bakery and had been with me since the beginning—actually laughed. Not unkindly. She said, "I wondered how long you'd keep this going. You've seemed miserable for at least a year."

A year. I'd spent a full year visibly miserable, and I was the last person to notice.

That's what the far green does. It traps you in the gap between where you are and where you thought you'd be, and you spend so much energy managing that cognitive dissonance that you stop noticing whether you're actually building anything.

Now, let me complicate this, because the opposite trap is just as real: there are people who never leave their familiar pasture even when it's genuinely exhausted. They stay in jobs that stopped growing them five years ago, or hold investments that stopped making sense two market cycles ago, and they call it "loyalty" or "consistency" when it's really just fear of the unknown.

How do you tell the difference?

Here's the framework I wish I'd had back then. I call it the Three Grounds test, and it's simple enough to remember but specific enough to actually use.

First Ground: Is this building compound value?

Compound value means your efforts stack. Every year you're here, you get better at being here, and that improvement multiplies what you built last year. A craftsman who's spent twenty years mastering a skill has compound value. A consultant hopping between clients with no repeat business, solving the same surface-level problems over and over, doesn't.

If you're not compounding—if year five feels the same as year two—you're probably on the wrong ground. Not because it's bad ground, but because you're not working it right, or it's not suited to you.

Second Ground: Does this align with how you actually want to spend your limited energy?

Notice I didn't say "passion." Passion is overrated. I'm asking: when you imagine yourself doing this work at 60, or 70, does it feel like a life you'd choose, or does it feel like time you're serving?

I loved the idea of consulting. I loved the story I could tell about being an independent expert. But I hated the actual work—the pitching, the hand-holding, the explaining the same concepts to clients who'd never implement them. The consulting practice aligned with my self-image but not with my actual energy. That mismatch is expensive. It leaks motivation every single day until you wake up and realize you've been running on fumes for years.

Third Ground: Are you staying out of conviction or sunk cost?

This is the brutal one. Strip away everything you've already invested—the time, the money, the identity you've built around this path. If you were starting from zero today, knowing what you know now, would you choose this ground again?

If the answer is no, you're farming sunk cost. And sunk cost is a crop that never yields.

Here's what I did wrong: I kept my consulting practice running because I couldn't face the idea that I'd built something that didn't work. The business itself was fine—it paid its bills, mostly—but it wasn't building toward anything. I wasn't getting better at it. I wasn't enjoying it more. I was just... there. Defending my past choice by refusing to make a new one.

By the time I finally admitted that, I'd burned through what could have been a year's worth of living expenses. Not because the business was losing money—it was just barely profitable—but because I wasn't paying myself. I was reinvesting everything into trying to make it feel like the opportunity I'd imagined it would be when I started. Marketing that didn't work. Systems I didn't need. A website redesign I thought would change everything.

You know what changed everything? Closing it down.

Within three months, I'd taken a full-time role doing work I'd been avoiding because I was "too busy" with the consulting practice. Within six months, I'd rebuilt the cash cushion. Within a year, I was doing better work, making more money, and sleeping through the night again.

The far green wasn't greener. It was just different. And different isn't always better—it's just different.

But here's the twist, and this is what the parable actually teaches if you read it closely: Osric didn't fail because he looked at the far ridge. He failed because he abandoned good ground without understanding what made it good. He saw greener grass and assumed that meant better grass, without asking *why* his current pasture worked.

The corrective isn't to never explore. It's to know your own ground well enough that you can evaluate whether new ground is actually better or just different.

So here's your Monday-morning action, and I mean this literally: Take fifteen minutes and write down what makes your current situation valuable. Not what it could be. Not what you wish it were. What it *is*, right now, that's working. The relationships, the knowledge, the systems, the reputation, the compounding advantage of being known and trusted in a specific context.

Then write down what you'd be giving up if you walked away. Be specific. Not "my career" or "my business"—actual concrete things. The client who always refers you. The skill you've spent five years developing. The network that knows your name.

Then—and only then—write down what the "greener grass" actually offers that your current ground doesn't.

If you're honest, you'll probably find one of three things:

One: The new opportunity offers something genuinely valuable that you can't get where you are, and the cost of switching is worth it. Great. Go. But go with your eyes open, knowing what you're trading.

Two: The new opportunity offers something you *want* but don't actually *need*, and the cost of switching is higher than you'd like to admit. In which case, maybe the real opportunity is learning to want what you have.

Three: The new opportunity offers the same things you already have, just in a different package, and you're only looking at it because you're bored or frustrated or scared. In which case, the problem isn't your pasture. It's that you've stopped tending it.

I was in category three for three solid years before I admitted it.

The far green shimmers because it's far. Distance erases the weeds, the rocks, the thin patches. Up close, every pasture has problems. The question isn't whether your pasture has problems—it's whether you know them well enough to work around them, and whether the work itself is building something you want to keep building.

That's not settling. That's strategy.

And if you find yourself defending a choice you stopped believing in—whether it's a business, a job, a investment approach, or any other path you've committed to—ask yourself: What would I do if admitting I was wrong cost me nothing?

Then do that.

Because the only thing more expensive than admitting you took a wrong turn three years ago is spending three *more* years refusing to turn around.

ELEVEN — The Measuring of Flocks

There is a kind of poverty that has nothing to do with the size of a flock and everything to do with what a shepherd has decided to measure it against, and it is, in my long experience keeping this valley's tallies, the single most common way a genuinely comfortable household talks itself into unnecessary hardship. No mountain, no storm, no sickness ever did as much damage to this particular family's fortune as one overheard sentence at a tavern table.

I have watched a version of this same trouble visit at least a dozen households in my years keeping this valley's tallies, always in some fresh disguise, always arriving from outside rather than from within — a stray comment, a market-day rumor, a single figure spoken aloud by someone who meant nothing by it and never learned what it cost. There were two shepherds, brothers by marriage rather than blood, whose flocks grazed adjoining land, and for the better part of twenty years neither had thought much about the size of the other's holdings, because each had grown his own at whatever pace his own ground and his own patience allowed. They had married sisters the same summer, built neighboring homesteads the same year, and raised their children together with the easy, unremarkable closeness of families who share a fence line and a well. If either man had ever felt competitive with the other, in all those years, he had never once shown it — their gatherings at each other's tables were frequent and genuinely warm, and their children grew up more like siblings than cousins.

The two men's wives, sisters raised in the same household, had always joked that they'd married their husbands partly because the men got along so easily with each other, sparing the family the strained holidays and divided loyalties that plagued other households where in-laws couldn't stand one another. The two families shared a well, traded labor freely during lambing and shearing without ever bothering to keep close account of who owed whom, and had raised their children to think of each other's homes as extensions of their own. It was, by any measure, exactly the kind of relationship a passing remark from a stranger ought to have been powerless to damage.

That changed the autumn the younger brother-in-law, Aodh, overheard a trader remark, in passing and without any particular weight behind it, at the tavern where half the valley's business was conducted over cider, that the elder brother-in-law's flock had grown to nearly twice the size of his own. The trader meant nothing by it — he was simply making conversation, comparing two of his regular customers the way traders idly compare anyone, with no more intent behind the remark than a comment on the weather.

Aodh had not, until that morning, felt poor. His flock fed his family, grew steadily, and had never once given him cause for complaint. He walked home that evening the same contented man he'd been the evening before, or told himself he did. But the number the trader mentioned — twice — lodged in him the way a splinter lodges, small and sharp and impossible to ignore once noticed, working its way slowly deeper the more he tried to stop thinking about it. He found himself, in the weeks after, counting his brother-in-law's flock from a distance whenever the two men's pastures came into view together, an exercise that told him nothing he didn't already sense but that he could not seem to stop doing. He began, for the first time in twenty years, to measure his own flock not against what it had been the year before, which was the only honest measure a flock has, but against a number belonging to someone else entirely.

His wife noticed the change in him before he could have named it himself — a new restlessness at the supper table, a habit of walking to the boundary fence some evenings just to look across at his brother-in-law's grazing land, a sharper tone than usual when she gently asked whether the new spending was entirely necessary. She raised the question directly, once, and he brushed it aside with an irritation that surprised them both, insisting the ewes were simply good business, an ordinary expansion any sensible shepherd would make given the chance. He believed this, mostly, in the moment he said it. He bought ewes he could not properly afford that winter, borrowing against a wool sale still months off, in an effort to close a gap that existed nowhere except in a passing remark he'd overheard and could not stop turning over. He grazed them on ground he had previously, wisely, left fallow every third year to recover, because fallow ground grows nothing to measure and he had, by then, stopped being able to think in any terms except the measuring.

A more experienced shepherd, seeing the state of the fallow ground that second spring, might have called a halt right then and cut his losses before the third year's thinner grass compounded the damage further, but Aodh was, by his own later admission, too embarrassed by then to reverse course openly, worried that undoing the purchase would only draw more attention to the very comparison he'd been trying so hard to escape in the first place. The new ewes strained pasture that had never been meant to carry that many animals at once. The fallow ground, grazed two years running instead of rested, gave thinner grass the second year, and thinner grass again the third. His flock, larger now on paper than it had ever been, was also hungrier, weaker, and carrying a debt against a wool sale that came in, that year, lighter than he'd counted on, because thin sheep grow thin wool.

He did not go under. But he spent four years afterward simply undoing what a single autumn's overheard remark had cost him — resting the ground back to health, paying down the debt, watching his flock shrink before it could grow properly again, this time on its own honest schedule. His wife, watching him those four years work harder for less than he'd worked in the twenty years before, asked him once, gently, what exactly he'd been chasing that autumn he bought the extra ewes, and he found, when he actually tried to answer her, that he could not name a single real thing he'd wanted from the larger flock beyond simply no longer being the smaller number in a comparison no one but he had ever been keeping.

Maren, called in that fourth year to help Aodh work out a repayment plan for the debt against his thinning wool sales, remembers asking him plainly, in the course of the accounting, what exactly he had wanted the larger flock to give him — more coin, certainly, but coin for what specific purpose, since his household had never lacked for its needs before the comparison took hold. Aodh sat with the question a long while before answering, and what he finally said stayed with Maren for years afterward as one of the truer things anyone had ever told her across a tally-stick. "I think I wanted to stop feeling like the smaller flock," he said. "Not richer. Not more comfortable. Just not smaller. And I never once asked myself what I'd actually have gained the day I finally wasn't, because there was never a day like that waiting for me. There was only ever the next number to catch up to."

When the two men's wives finally compared notes on the whole affair, years after it was resolved, they discovered between them a small, private irony neither had shared with the other at the time — Aodh's sister-in-law admitted that she herself had gone through a similar quiet season of comparison a decade earlier, over some other passing remark long since forgotten, and had never once mentioned it to her husband either, having worked her own way out of it privately before it did any lasting damage to their finances. The elder brother-in-law, for his part, had never once compared his own flock to Aodh's, had no idea the remark had even been made, and would have been baffled — was baffled, when Aodh finally told him the whole of it, years later — to learn that a stranger's passing comment about a number had cost his brother-in-law four years of real, patient growth.

"He wasn't racing me," Aodh told Maren. "He didn't know there was a race. I built the whole track myself, ran it alone, and lost to a runner who was never on it."

The flock you compare yourself to is very often not competing with you at all — it is simply grazing its own ground, at its own pace, indifferent to the number you've assigned it in your mind. A fortune measured against your own past is a fortune you can grow honestly. A fortune measured against someone else's present is a fortune you will eventually borrow against, badly, to chase a finish line only you believe exists.

Aodh and his brother-in-law grew old together on their adjoining land, as close in their final years as they'd been at the start, and Aodh made a point, every so often, of telling the story on himself at gatherings, laughing at his own younger foolishness in a way that Maren always found more instructive than any solemn warning could have been. The next story turns from a fortune undone by comparison to a fortune undone by something quieter still — a man's plain unwillingness to admit that a costly choice had already cost him everything it was going to.

TWELVE — The Ram That Would Not Be Culled

There is a particular stubbornness that has nothing to do with strength of character and everything to do with the simple, human unwillingness to admit that a costly decision has already cost what it is going to cost. I have watched this stubbornness ruin more flocks, more households, and more good men's judgment than any storm the mountain has ever produced, and Brogan's ram is the story the valley tells to name it plainly.

Every flock keeps, at its center, one or two rams whose bloodline sets the character of every lamb born for years afterward, and a shepherd's judgment about which rams to keep and which to cull is, more than almost any other single decision, the decision that determines what a flock becomes.

A shepherd named Brogan had bought, as a young man, at no small expense, a ram of unusually good size and bearing from a trader passing through — the finest animal he had ever owned, and the foundation, he was certain, of a bloodline that would carry his flock's reputation for a generation. He had gone into debt to buy it, a debt that took him three years to clear, and had told everyone who would listen, in those first years, that he had never spent coin better in his life. The ram stood a head taller at the shoulder than any other in the valley, carried itself with a bearing other shepherds openly admired at market, and Brogan had, by his own later admission, fallen a little in love with the animal in the particular way a man sometimes falls in love with the single best decision he believes he has ever made. The trader who sold him the ram was long gone by the time the flaw appeared, having passed through only that one season on his way to markets further south, and Brogan sometimes wondered, in his later years, whether the man had known something of the bloodline's hidden weakness and simply moved on before it could be discovered — a suspicion he could never prove and eventually let go of, since it changed nothing about the four years he himself had chosen to keep the ram after the flaw was plain to see.

Other shepherds in the valley, seeing the ram's early offspring at market, began asking to breed their own ewes to him, paying Brogan a modest fee for the privilege, and for those first six years the arrangement burnished his reputation as thoroughly as it filled his purse, with several neighboring flocks carrying at least a partial line back to the animal he'd bought as a young man on nothing more than a trader's word and his own sharp eye. The ram sired excellent lambs for six years. In the seventh, it began throwing offspring with a weakness in the legs that showed only after a lamb's first hard winter — sound-looking at birth, sound through spring and summer, and then, come the first real cold, buckling in a way that could not be fed or nursed out of them. His wife noticed it before he fully allowed himself to, remarking one evening, with the particular bluntness a spouse is permitted, that the ram's lambs seemed to favor a leg more often than any other sire's did, an observation he brushed off gently at the time but found himself returning to, uneasily, in the months that followed. He mentioned the losses, those first two winters, to a handful of neighbors almost casually, the way a man mentions any ordinary run of bad luck, and none of them thought much of it either, since every flock absorbed the occasional unlucky season without it meaning anything about the animals' underlying quality. Two lambs that winter. Four the next. Brogan told himself, that second winter, that four losses out of a flock that size was still an ordinary enough misfortune, the kind every shepherd absorbed from time to time without it meaning anything larger. By the ram's ninth year, better than a third of its offspring carried the flaw, and it was, by then, unmistakably the ram, not chance, not feed, not any of the explanations Brogan reached for first, each one a little less convincing than the last even to himself.

His wife, who had watched the flock's tallies as closely as he had over their years together, was the first to say the word aloud in their own kitchen — cull it — and Brogan's reaction to hearing it from someone he trusted so completely was, to his own later shame, worse than his reaction to any neighbor's advice had been, a flash of genuine anger that surprised them both and that he apologized for within the hour, though the apology did nothing to change his mind about the ram itself. Every shepherd who saw his flock told him the same thing, plainly and without much diplomacy: the ram had to go. Cull it, breed from younger stock, stop the flaw from spreading further into a bloodline that would otherwise carry it for another decade of lambs.

Brogan would not do it. He had paid more for that ram than for any animal before or since, had built his flock's whole reputation on its early years, and could not, even faced with the mounting evidence of what it was now doing to his lambs, bring himself to treat the animal as anything other than the prize he had once been so certain it was. To cull the ram, he found himself feeling in some part of his mind he was ashamed of, would be to admit that the debt he'd carried three hard years to pay off, the pride he'd carried since, the whole story he told about the ram at markets and shearings, had all been spent on a mistake — and that admission felt, to him, like a larger loss than any number of lambs. He told himself, each winter, that the losses were an unlucky season, a bad batch of feed, anything other than the plain thing every other shepherd could already see. There was, in those four years, a particular autumn that Brogan himself later singled out as the moment he might still have changed course cheaply, before the cost had grown as large as it eventually did — a season in which the losses briefly plateaued rather than climbed, and he allowed himself to believe, for the length of that one deceptively quiet winter, that the worst had already passed and the ram might yet prove sound after all. It hadn't, and it didn't, and the following winter's losses, worse than any before them, put the lie to that brief hope more thoroughly than any single bad season could have on its own. He kept the ram four years past the point at which every honest measure said to let it go, and in those four years watched the flaw spread from a third of its offspring to nearly half, weakening a bloodline that would, by the time he finally relented, take a decade of careful breeding to clean back out.

Brogan's own son, watching all of this unfold as a boy of twelve or thirteen, later became one of the more disciplined breeders the valley had seen in a generation, and he traced the discipline directly back to those four extra years of watching his father's pride cost the family more than any single bad decision reasonably should have. "I used to think the lesson was about the ram," he told Maren once, long after his father had passed. "It wasn't. The ram was just an animal that got sick in a particular way. The lesson was watching a good, sensible man become unable to see plain arithmetic the moment his own pride sat on top of it. I've never trusted my own judgment completely since, on anything I've already spent heavily on. I always ask someone else to look at the numbers first, someone who didn't pay for the ram."

It was not, in the end, a neighbor's advice that changed his mind, though he'd heard plenty of it and ignored all of it. It was Maren herself, then younger, going over the valley's yearly tallies with him and simply reading the numbers aloud in order — six good years, then a line of losses climbing steadily upward with nothing else in the flock's care that had changed to explain them except the one thing he would not name.

"You already paid for the ram," she told him. "That coin is spent and gone no matter what you do now. The only question left is how many more winters you're willing to pay, in lambs, to avoid admitting the first payment didn't turn out the way you hoped."

He culled the ram that season, walking it to the far pasture himself rather than sending a hired hand, a small private ceremony of accountability that no one but Maren ever knew the reason for. Several of the shepherds who had bred their own ewes to the ram in its good early years came to Brogan that same season, once word spread that he'd finally culled it, quietly asking after the animal's offspring in their own flocks and beginning, in their own smaller ways, the same slow work of breeding the flaw back out that Brogan himself was undertaking — a ripple of correction that spread, in time, to nearly every flock in that end of the valley that had ever carried a trace of the bloodline. It took him, as the other shepherds had warned him it would, most of a decade to breed the weakness back out of his flock — a decade that would have been half as long had he acted the first winter the flaw appeared, rather than the fifth. He told the story often in his later years, always to young shepherds facing some decision of their own they seemed reluctant to make, and always ended it the same way: "Ask yourself what you'd do if you'd never spent a single coin on the thing in front of you. Whatever answer you give, that's the honest one — the coin already spent has no vote in it."

What you have already spent on a thing does not obligate the future to keep spending alongside it. The coin, the years, the pride bound up in the first decision — all of it is gone the moment it's spent, regardless of what you decide next, and the only honest question left is what the thing in front of you is worth now, not what you once believed it would become. Brogan did not lose four extra years to a ram. He lost them to his own reluctance to admit the ram had already cost him what it was going to cost.

Brogan's grandchildren still tell the story of the ram at their own hearths now, and it has become, in the way these things happen, something close to a byword in that end of the valley — "keeping the ram," people say, when they mean a man too proud to admit a costly mistake, and most who use the phrase these days have long since forgotten whose ram it originally was. The story that follows is, in its way, the ram's story turned inside out — not a stubbornness that keeps too much, but a softness that keeps too much, for reasons that feel, in the moment, like the opposite of pride.

THIRTEEN — The Culling Song

The narrow-hipped ewe stood at the edge of the fold, and Isolde's hand hesitated on the gate latch.

She'd already walked past this animal twice that morning. Her mother sat on the fence rail twenty feet away, saying nothing, which was worse than any lecture. The ewe wasn't sick. Wasn't lame. Had a good coat, bright eyes, ate well. But those hips—Isolde had watched her struggle through lambing the previous spring, watched her strain and heave while the other ewes delivered without drama. The lamb had been small. The ewe had recovered slowly.

"Keep the strong, keep the sound, send the rest before the ground goes hard."

The valley's culling song. Every shepherd knew it. Isolde's mother had sung it with a matter-of-factness that seemed almost brutal when Isolde was young—no emotion in her voice, just steady purpose. But her eyes, Isolde remembered, had never left the animals. She watched everything.

Isolde's hand dropped from the latch.

"I can give her another year," she said, not quite looking at her mother. "She might strengthen. Some do."

Her mother didn't answer right away. When she did, her voice was quiet. "You're allowed to feel that. Just don't let the feeling hold the gate."

I'm going to be honest about something, though I should probably just give you the tidy advice and move on: I spent years telling people to be ruthless with their finances. Cut the subscriptions you don't use. Eliminate the habits that drain your account. Build the portfolio that optimizes returns. And then one day I looked at my own spreadsheet—the one where I tracked every dollar—and realized I hadn't enjoyed a meal out in six months because I couldn't stop calculating the compound interest I was losing.

The advice was right. The life it created was miserable.

So when I talk about culling—and yes, we're still talking about money here, not just sheep—I'm not going to pretend it's simple. The hard part isn't knowing what to cut. The hard part is that the things you need to cut often feel like kindness. Like hope. Like giving yourself (or someone you care about) a chance.

Isolde made the cut that morning. Sent the ewe to market with the others who wouldn't make it through another winter. It felt awful. For three days afterward, she second-guessed herself every time she walked past the fold.

But here's what happened the next spring.

The ewes who remained lambed early and easily. Strong lambs, vigorous from birth. Isolde had more wool to sell because she wasn't nursing weak animals through recovery. She had more time because she wasn't treating problems that should never have existed in the first place. And—this was the part that surprised her—she slept better. The low-grade anxiety that had hummed in the background all winter, the constant wondering if this ewe or that ram would make it through, was gone.

The flock was smaller. But it was sound.

Now let's talk about your actual money, because the metaphor only gets you so far.

You probably have something in your financial life right now that you know—if you're being honest with yourself—isn't working. Maybe it's:

A subscription service you signed up for with good intentions (you were going to learn the language, finally get in shape, read all those books) that you haven't used in four months but keep paying for because canceling feels like admitting defeat.

A side project or investment you put money into that hasn't returned anything close to what you hoped, but you keep funding it because you've already put in so much that walking away feels like waste.

A relationship pattern—lending money to the same person, covering the same emergencies, funding the same promises—that you maintain because saying no feels cruel.

A house that's too big, a car payment that's too high, a lifestyle that looked reasonable when you set it up but now quietly drains you every month.

Here's what that costs you, and I don't mean just the dollars:

Every month you keep paying for the gym membership you don't use, you're not just losing $50. You're maintaining a story about yourself that isn't true. You're the person who goes to the gym.

Except you're not. And every time that charge hits your account, you feel it—a little flicker of guilt, a little reminder of the gap between who you think you are and who you actually are. That has a price. It accumulates.

Every year you hold an investment that's underperforming because selling feels like failure, you're not just accepting poor returns. You're teaching yourself that sunk costs matter more than future opportunity. You're rehearsing the story that changing your mind means you were wrong. And that story will cost you in every other decision you make.

Every time you lend money you know won't come back, you're not being kind. You're buying distance from a hard conversation. And that distance compounds. The relationship doesn't get closer because you keep saying yes. It gets harder to talk about the real things.

The culling song isn't about cruelty. It's about refusing to let misplaced kindness bleed you dry.

Isolde's daughter learned to cull the year she turned sixteen. Isolde made her do it alone—walked her through the reasoning beforehand, answered her questions, but wouldn't stand at the gate with her when the moment came.

"You'll want me there," Isolde told her. "You'll want someone else to confirm the decision, or to override you, or to share the blame. But this is your flock. And if you can't make this call by yourself, you'll never trust that you made the right one."

Her daughter sent a ram lamb to market that day—beautiful animal, rare coloring, the kind of coat that would've drawn attention at any fair. But his frame was light. His legs were too fine. He wouldn't have survived a hard winter, and breeding him would've passed those weaknesses down.

She cried afterward. Isolde didn't tell her not to.

"The hard part," she said instead, "isn't that it feels bad. The hard part is that doing the right thing doesn't make the bad feeling go away. You just have to know it was still right."

To be honest—and here I go again, contradicting myself—there's a version of this advice that's too harsh. I've watched people take the idea of ruthless optimization and turn it into a kind of punishment. They cut everything. They eliminate joy. They build a budget so tight there's no room for being human.

That's not what I'm talking about.

The culling song isn't about minimalism. It's not about living on the smallest amount possible or proving how disciplined you can be. It's about looking at what you're actually carrying and asking: Does this make the flock stronger, or am I keeping it because I'm afraid to let go?

There's a difference.

The subscription you actually use, the one that genuinely makes your life better three times a week? Keep it. You don't get points for suffering.

The investment that's underperforming but fits a part of your strategy you've thought through and still believe in? Fine. Hold it.

Not every position pays off immediately.

The person you're helping who's actually using the help to build something real? That's not a leak. That's a choice.

But the things you're keeping out of fear, out of guilt, out of the story you're telling yourself about who you should be—those will hollow you out. And you'll wake up one day with a flock that looks full but can't make it through winter.

Isolde didn't become beloved in the valley because her flock was the largest. She became the shepherd other shepherds asked for advice because her flock was sound. Year after year, her animals were strong. Her lambs were vigorous. She had fewer catastrophes, fewer emergencies, fewer nights spent treating problems that shouldn't have existed.

And here's the thing nobody talks about: she had more peace.

Not because everything was easy. Because she'd already made the hard calls. She wasn't lying awake wondering if she should've cut something two seasons ago. She wasn't carrying the weight of decisions she'd avoided. She'd done the work. And that work had bought her something you can't get any other way: the ability to stop second-guessing herself.

You can't buy that. You can't optimize your way into it. You can only earn it by doing the thing that feels hard now so you don't have to carry the weight of not doing it later.

So here's what you do Monday morning.

Not someday. Not when you feel ready. Monday.

Open your bank statement—the full one, every charge from the last three months. Not just the big expenses. All of it.

Find one thing you've been paying for that you know isn't working. Not the thing that's easiest to cut. The thing that carries the most guilt. The one you've been avoiding looking at because acknowledging it means admitting something about yourself you don't want to face.

Cancel it.

And here's the part that matters: Don't replace it with something else. Don't use the money you save to add another subscription or cover another expense. Just let it go. Let there be empty space where that charge used to be.

Sit with how that feels.

Because what you're going to notice—maybe not the first week, but soon—is that the relief doesn't come from having more money. It comes from no longer maintaining a story that wasn't true. It comes from the gap closing between who you think you are and what you're actually doing.

That's the culling song. Not the moment you make the cut. The breath you take afterward when you realize you're not carrying that weight anymore.

Isolde's last autumn, she walked the fold with her granddaughter, a girl of twelve who asked too many questions and challenged every answer.

"Why do we have to send them away?" the girl asked, watching the drover's cart disappear down the valley road. "Why can't we just keep them all and figure it out?"

Isolde didn't answer right away. She watched the cart until it rounded the bend and disappeared.

"Because figuring it out," she said finally, "means something dies slowly instead of quickly. And I've never found a kindness in that."

The girl thought about this. "But what if you're wrong? What if the one you sent away was stronger than you thought?"

"Then I was wrong," Isolde said. "And I'll be wrong again. But I'd rather be wrong making a decision than wrong because I couldn't."

The girl didn't look satisfied. Isolde didn't expect her to. Some things you can only understand by standing at the gate yourself, hand on the latch, knowing what comes next.

The question you're carrying isn't whether to cull. You already know what needs to go. You've known for a while.

The question is whether you trust yourself enough to stop waiting for permission.

FOURTEEN — The Long Winter

The Faolains kept three years of hay in their barn. Everyone knew this. Most of us kept one year's worth, maybe eighteen months if we'd had a good season and wanted to play it safe. The Faolains kept three.

I remember the first time I saw inside their barn—I was maybe nineteen, helping Declan Faolain haul in the last of an August cutting. The stacks went back farther than I'd imagined, row after row disappearing into the dimness at the rear. "Your father planning for the apocalypse?" I'd asked, trying to keep it light. Declan had just shrugged. "He says if you're not scared, you're not paying attention."

At the time I'd thought that was paranoid. My own father kept a year's worth, sometimes fifteen months, and we'd never lost animals to a hard winter. We were prudent people. We planned. The Faolains, though—they seemed to live under a private cloud of dread the rest of us couldn't see.

This was 2009, maybe early 2010. The economy had just cratered, though that felt distant from our valley. We weren't leveraged. We didn't have subprime mortgages on our pastureland. The financial crisis was something that happened to other people, people who'd been greedy or careless or both. We told ourselves we were insulated.

Then the winter of 2011 hit.

It started normal enough—first snow in early November, temperatures dropping steadily through December. By January we knew we were in for a long haul, but nothing catastrophic. February, though. February was when things turned.

The pass closed on the eighth. Not unusual—it closed most winters for a week or two when the drifts got too deep for the plows to keep up. But this time it didn't reopen. A week became two weeks became a month. The valley's only road connection to the outside world was a forty-foot wall of snow that kept building every time the highway crews tried to cut through.

I remember standing in Morrison's feed store in late February—this was maybe the fifteenth or sixteenth, I'm not great with exact dates—and watching Jim Morrison do math on the back of a receipt. He sold feed and hay to everyone in the valley. He knew everyone's stock counts, knew their consumption rates. "If this goes past March tenth," he said, not looking up from his calculations, "we're going to have a problem."

By early March, people were starting to make choices. Cull the herd now while the animals still had some weight on them, or gamble that the pass would open and hang on to your breeding stock? Some folks slaughtered everything down to their core breeding pairs and salted the meat. Others borrowed hay from neighbors who'd had good years, promising to pay it back double next season.

The Faolains didn't do either.

I ran into Declan in Morrison's—this would've been March seventh or eighth, right around when Jim's deadline was starting to feel real—and he was buying salt blocks. Not selling off stock, not panic-buying feed. Just picking up salt blocks like it was an ordinary spring.

"How're you fixed for hay?" I asked him.

"We're fine," he said. Not defensive, not boastful. Just fine.

"You selling any? Because Morrison's about tapped out and—"

"We're not selling."

That should've been my first clue, but I was young and still thought being clever meant being optimized. I'd kept exactly fourteen months of hay going into winter. We were in month four. I had ten months left. The math worked as long as the pass opened by April, which it always had. Every winter in recorded history, the pass had opened by mid-April at the latest.

This is the part where I should tell you I saw the writing on the wall and made smart decisions. I didn't. I sat tight and told myself the Faolains were paranoid and I was rational and everything would work out because it always had.

The pass opened April twenty-third.

We'd been cut off for seventy-four days. I had three weeks of hay left when the first trucks came through. My neighbor, Cullane—good guy, ran about twice as many sheep as I did—had been out for eight days. He'd kept his breeding ewes alive by feeding them meal mixed with sawdust and hoping they wouldn't starve before relief came. They didn't starve, but half of them lost their lambs that spring. Stress, malnutrition, take your pick.

The Faolains never even got close to the line. When I helped Declan with lambing that year—he needed extra hands because their flock had come through so healthy—I asked him how much hay they'd had left when the pass finally opened.

"About eighteen months' worth," he said.

They'd burned through half their reserve. Their supposedly excessive, irrational, paranoid reserve. And they'd still had a year and a half left over.

Now here's where most financial advice would tell you: build a three-year emergency fund, maintain excess capacity, always prepare for the worst-case scenario. And look, that's not wrong. But it's also not the point.

The point is this: I spent that entire winter afraid. Not terrified, not panicking—I'm not trying to be dramatic—but carrying this low-grade constant fear that I'd miscalculated. Every morning I'd go out to the barn and look at the depleting stacks and run the math again. How many sheep, how much consumption per day, how many days until the hay ran out, how long could I stretch it if I started cutting rations, at what point would I have to start making permanent decisions about animals I'd spent years breeding.

Declan didn't carry that fear. I saw him almost every day that winter—valley closed in on itself, everyone running into everyone else at the post office or the store—and he never had that look. You know the look I mean if you've ever been genuinely worried about money. That thing behind your eyes that's always calculating, always running scenarios.

The Faolains had bought their way out of fear three years earlier, when they'd stacked that "excessive" hay. The cost was storage space and capital tied up in feed that might never get used. The return was seventy-four days of sleeping through the night while the rest of us ran the math over and over.

Most financial advice treats wealth-building like a game you can win—maximize returns, optimize asset allocation, calculate your risk tolerance to three decimal places. I used to think that way too. Spent my twenties reading books about investment strategies and trying to figure out the perfect savings rate and telling myself that being smart about money meant being precise about money.

The Long Winter taught me something different. The real goal isn't winning the game. The real goal is to stop being afraid of money early enough that you can actually enjoy the years you have left.

Though I should say—and this is going to sound like it contradicts what I just told you—I still don't keep three years of hay. I keep about twenty months' worth now, sometimes two years if it's been a good season. That's where I landed after that winter, and it's probably not optimal by either standard. The Faolains would tell you it's not enough. My younger self would tell you it's inefficient capital allocation.

But I sleep fine. That's the whole calculation right there. I sleep fine, and I stopped running the math in my head every morning, and when feed prices spike or a dry summer cuts the hay yield, I feel it but I don't fear it. That's worth something. I'm not sure how you'd quantify it in a spreadsheet, but it's worth something.

Here's what you can actually do with this, because philosophy without action is just expensive decoration:

Go look at your bank balance right now—I mean actually pull it up, don't estimate—and ask yourself how long you could maintain your current life if your income stopped tomorrow. Not your "stripped down to bare essentials" life. Your actual current life. The one you're living.

If the answer makes your chest tight, you know what to do. You start building the reserve. Not because some book told you that six months of expenses is the rule, and not because you're optimizing for the statistically most likely emergency scenario. You build it because carrying that fear around costs you something every single day, and at some point the cost of the fear exceeds the cost of the insurance.

How much is enough? I don't know. That's the honest answer. The Faolains would tell you three years. The standard advice says six months. I think it's however much it takes for you to stop doing the math in your head when you wake up at three in the morning.

The other thing—and this is harder to action-plan because it's not about money directly—is that you have to get comfortable with other people thinking you're paranoid. The Faolains took ten years of being the weird family with too much hay in their barn before that winter proved them right. Ten years of people making jokes, asking pointed questions about storage costs, suggesting they were tying up capital that could be "working for them" elsewhere.

They never defended it. They just kept stacking hay. And when the crisis came—because eventually the crisis always comes, even if it's not the crisis you prepared for—they had what they needed and the rest of us didn't.

I'm not naturally built like that. I want people to think I'm making smart choices. I want to explain my reasoning and have it validated. Took me most of my thirties to get comfortable with the idea that what looks like prudence to me might look like waste to someone else, and that's fine. Their opinion of my reserves doesn't keep me warm when the pass closes.

One more thing, then I'll let you go: the winter eventually ended. The pass opened, trucks came through, feed prices went back to normal. Life resumed. And because life resumed, because the crisis ended, it became very easy to tell yourself it had been an anomaly. A once-in-a-lifetime event. A statistical outlier.

The Faolains didn't rebuild their three-year reserve immediately. They couldn't—they'd burned through half of it, and you can't replace eighteen months of hay in a single growing season. It took them four years to get back to three years' worth.

Four years of being "inefficient" again. Four years of capital tied up in hay that just sat there, doing nothing, earning nothing. Four years of people forgetting the Long Winter and going back to their optimized one-year reserves.

The pass closed for sixty-one days in the winter of 2018.

I don't know if Declan still keeps three years of hay—I moved out of the valley in 2020, chasing cheaper land farther south—but I'd bet money he does. Because the thing about buying your way out of fear is that it only works if you stay bought out. The minute you decide the crisis is over and you can optimize again, you're back in the game. Back to running the math. Back to that feeling behind your eyes.

Optimization is the enemy of peace. I believe that now in a way I couldn't have before that winter. Every bit of excess capacity you build into your life is capacity you're not squeezing for maximum return, and someone somewhere has a spreadsheet that proves you're leaving money on the table.

They're right. You are leaving money on the table.

The question is whether the money you're leaving is worth less than the fear you're not carrying.

FIFTEEN — The Borrowed Ram

I still have the thank-you card on my desk. Floral border, pre-printed "With Gratitude" in gold script, and underneath it, in her careful elementary-teacher handwriting: *Thank you for helping me see that real estate really is different this time. Looking forward to my rental income years!* Her name was Ellen Pritchard. Third-grade teacher. Three years from retirement in 2006 when she walked into my office with a question about whether she should use some of her savings to buy a second rental property, and I — twenty-nine years old, two years into selling mortgages, riding the best market I'd ever seen and convinced it was the new normal — told her yes. Told her the fundamentals had changed. Told her that waiting was the risk, not buying.

She put forty percent of what she had into a down payment on a duplex in a neighborhood that was, I told her, "on the upswing." Eighteen months later the market turned and she couldn't cover both mortgages when one unit sat empty for five months straight and the tenants in the other unit stopped paying and wouldn't leave. She lost the down payment. Postponed retirement by four years. Went back to teaching with the kind of smile that doesn't reach the eyes anymore, the smile you learn when you've spent a career getting eight-year-olds to believe that effort matters and fairness exists, and then life teaches you the opposite on your own dime.

I keep the card because I should. Because the advice I gave her wasn't just wrong, it was the expensive kind of wrong — the kind that comes from mistaking one good year for a permanent condition and building a plan on the best-case story instead of the one that holds up when things go sideways. I didn't lie to her. I believed what I told her. That's worse, in some ways. You can't fix a lie by meaning well.

I tell you this because I want you to understand, before we go any further, that I know what it costs to borrow against a future you don't control. I've watched it cost someone else four years of their life. And the thing is, borrowing itself wasn't the mistake. Ellen could have borrowed and come out fine, the way thousands of other people did. The mistake was in how much of her security she staked on the best outcome arriving on schedule, and how little room she left herself for the version of the future that didn't cooperate.

There's a saying I heard from my grandmother, who heard it from someone whose name I've lost: *A rented ram breeds twice as many lambs as an owned one, and half as much peace.* I've thought about that line more in the fifteen years since Ellen's duplex went under than I did in all the years before it. Not because I deal in livestock — I don't — but because the truth it's pointing at is the same whether you're borrowing a ram or borrowing money or borrowing against your own future earnings to buy something today that you're betting tomorrow-you will be able to afford.

Let me tell you about two men who came to the same lending post the same spring, in a year when the frost broke early and the grass came up sweet and the world looked, for a moment, like a place where a young man with a small flock and large hopes might grow one into the other without waiting the twenty years his father had waited.

Their names were Tobin and Wick. Sons of small flock-holders, both. Each had just inherited a dozen ewes — not enough to live on, not yet, but enough to start from if a man was smart and didn't get unlucky and made the right choices about what to borrow and when. If you'd stood them side by side that morning at the lending post you would've said they were more alike than not. Same age, same station, same hunger. The kind of hunger you see in young men who've watched their fathers stay small and careful all their lives and have decided, privately, that they will not.

The lending post in those days was kept by a woman named Ivy Coates. She owned three prize rams of good Marlstone blood and she'd let them out to cover another man's ewes for a season in exchange for a share of the lambs that came of it. One lamb in three if you paid something down. One lamb in two if you wanted to pay nothing now and take the whole risk on credit, betting that the lambs would come and you'd have enough to cover what you owed and still come out ahead.

It was, in its way, no different from what Ellen did when she took out that second mortgage. You're borrowing against increase that doesn't exist yet. The lambs aren't born. The tenants haven't signed the lease. The market hasn't held. You're making a promise to your future self that your present self has no standing to make, and the terms of that promise will come due whether the future cooperates or not.

Tobin came to Ivy's post first. He asked her — and I like this about him, it's the question Ellen never thought to ask me — what her rams sired in a *bad* year. Not the average year. Not the best year she'd ever seen. The year when everything that could go wrong did. Ivy, who liked a man who asked that question, told him true: two lambs in three ewes in a fair season, one lamb in three when the winter ran long and the fodder gave out and half the ewes came up barren or lost what they were carrying.

Tobin sat with that awhile. Chewed a grass stem. Then he borrowed against six of his twelve ewes, not all twelve. Took Ivy's ram for a single season on the one-in-three share, paid down. He wanted, he said, to see what the ram gave him before he borrowed more than he could cover twice over even if the worst year he could imagine arrived on schedule.

Wick came that same afternoon. He asked what the *most* any man had ever gotten off Ivy's ram was. What the record was. The outlier. Ivy told him: one year, exceptional luck, near enough three lambs in four ewes. Wick heard that number and built his whole plan on it. Borrowed the ram against all twelve ewes, on the one-in-two credit share, nothing paid down. He figured that if the ram gave him even half of that record year he'd double his flock in a season and pay Ivy back in lambs he'd barely miss.

You see the shape of the mistake already. You might even be thinking, *Well, of course that's dumb, anyone can see that.* And yes, from here, with the story already told and the outcome already known, it looks obvious. But I want you to sit for a second in the place Wick was sitting when he made that call. Young. Hungry. Watching his father's flock stay the same size for thirty years while other men's flocks grew. Hearing about a year when someone else's bet paid off three-to-four. Thinking, *Why not me? Why shouldn't I be the one who gets the good year?*

That's not stupidity. That's hope. And hope, when it's wired directly into a contract you can't back out of, is one of the most expensive feelings there is.

The first year favored them both. The grass held. The ewes lambed well. Tobin's six ewes gave him eight lambs. He owed Ivy two, kept six, and sat down that autumn by lamplight and did his sums and saw that he'd grown his flock by half in a single season, owed nothing further, and had — maybe most importantly — learned the shape of what borrowing cost him. What it felt like to owe someone lambs that hadn't been born yet, and then to watch them be born, and then to hand them over. So the second year he borrowed again, but this time against nine ewes, not twelve. He'd grown cautious with success, not bold. Paid down what he owed as it came due, in lambs, before he ever thought about what he'd do with the rest.

Wick's twelve ewes gave him seventeen lambs that first year. Better than Tobin's, on the face of it. He crowed about it at the common fold in a way that made the older men look sideways at each other and say nothing, because they'd seen this part before and they knew what came next but also knew that a young man has to learn some things the way a lamb learns a fence — by running into it.

Wick owed Ivy eight lambs. Seventeen divides awkwardly, and she was owed the larger share of the odd one. After he paid her he still had nine lambs clear, which was more than Tobin's six, and he took that as proof that his judgment was the sounder of the two.

What Wick didn't reckon — because reckoning is slow and he was not a slow man — was that he'd also promised Ivy a cut of next year's flock. He'd doubled down, flush with his first-year success, and borrowed again on the same one-in-two terms, reasoning that a ram that gave him seventeen from twelve would give him something near that again from twenty. Ivy didn't talk him out of it. I asked her once, years later, why not. She said she'd told him the true numbers at the start, and a woman can't live a man's caution for him. Can only offer him the arithmetic and let him choose what to do with it.

The second year the snow came in the third week of lambing and stayed eleven days. Ewes that should've delivered easy and warm delivered into cold that killed a fair portion of what was born before it ever stood.

Tobin's nine ewes gave him seven lambs. A poor year. He owed Ivy three, kept four. Thin, but he could stand inside it without his knees buckling, because he'd never promised more than a thin year could cover.

Wick's twenty ewes gave him eleven lambs. Bad luck, but the worse blow was what he owed. He'd promised Ivy half his flock on the strength of a plenty that didn't come. The share he owed was reckoned against the number of ewes he'd bred, not the number of lambs that lived. When the snow took what it took, Wick owed Ivy more lambs than the season had given him.

He had borrowed against a future that did not arrive. And there is no ram living, however fine his blood, that can sire lambs enough to pay for a winter that's already happened.

It took Wick four years to climb out. He did climb out — he wasn't a fool, just impatient, and impatience, given enough winters, will sometimes teach itself into patience the hard way. But he had to sell off two ewes he'd owned outright, animals that owed nothing to anyone, just to make good on lambs he'd promised out of a flock that never grew as large as he'd convinced himself it would.

Tobin kept borrowing, season after season, in his small deliberate way. Never took more than his worst winter could cover twice over. By the time his hair went grey his flock had grown to four times its start. He owed no one. Had a name in the valley for a man whose word on a debt could be built on.

I saw them both years later, old men at the same shearing, and Wick said — not unkindly — that he'd always thought the difference between them was luck. Tobin shrugged. Said luck had visited them both, good and bad, in near enough equal measure. The difference, if there was one, was that he'd never let the good luck set the terms for what he owed.

Though I should say — and I mean this, because it's the part I got wrong with Ellen — that knowing this in your head and living it in your actual financial life are not the same thing. I knew, even in 2006, that real estate could go down. I'd seen the history. Read the books. But I was sitting in a market that had done nothing but go up for five years straight, and when you're inside that, when every client who bought two years ago has already made money and every client who waited is now priced out of the neighborhood they wanted, it gets very hard to give advice based on the bad year you've only read about instead of the good year you're watching happen in real time.

I'm not trying to excuse what I told Ellen. I'm trying to say that the mistake Wick made — borrowing against the best outcome instead of the worst — is not a mistake that only happens to impatient people, or to people who don't know better. It's a mistake that happens when the present is good enough, and loud enough, that it drowns out your ability to imagine the version of the future where things go badly and you're still on the hook for what you promised.

Borrowed money — borrowed stock, borrowed anything — can carry you forward faster than your own increase ever would. That part is true. Tobin proved it. He used Ivy's rams and grew his flock four times over in a span of years that would've taken him twice as long on his own. But the terms he set for himself were the terms that held up when the winter came and the lambs didn't. He never borrowed more than the worst year he could honestly imagine would let him repay.

Wick borrowed more than that. Not because he was reckless. Because he let one good year reset his sense of what the future owed him.

I think about Ellen sometimes, about whether she'd have made a different call if I'd asked her the question Ivy asked Tobin: *What happens if the bad year comes? Not the average year. The bad one. Can you still cover what you owe?* I don't know. Maybe she'd have bought the duplex anyway. Maybe she'd have sized down, bought something smaller, kept more cash in reserve. Maybe she'd have decided the risk wasn't worth it and stayed in the smaller life she already had, and been fine, and never known what she'd avoided.

What I know is I didn't ask. I told her about the good years instead. And the good years were real — they just weren't a promise.

The question I want you to sit with, before you borrow against anything — whether it's a loan, or a job you're counting on, or a raise you think is coming, or a market you're sure will hold — is this: *What do I owe if the thing I'm betting on doesn't arrive?* Not what do I owe if everything goes to plan. What do I owe if it doesn't. And can I live inside that answer without losing what I can't afford to lose.

Because the future you're borrowing against hasn't happened yet. The lambs aren't born. The tenant hasn't moved in. The promotion isn't yours. And if you've built the terms of your promise around the version of the future that you want, instead of the version you can survive, then you're not borrowing. You're betting. And the house you're betting against is time, and chance, and a world that has never, not once, promised any of us that good years arrive on schedule just because we need them to.

SIXTEEN — The Insurance of the Common Barn

There is a stretch of years in any life when nothing much happens, and I think we mistake this for safety. I have kept the tally-stones long enough now to know better. Nothing much happening is only the ordinary shape of waiting, and somewhere in it a slide is loosening on a slope, or a sickness is deciding which fold to visit first. I did not understand this the year Torvald Ren came down from the high pasture with two hundred sheep and buried a hundred and eighty of them under the mountain within the space of one bad afternoon, but I understood it well enough by the year's end, and so did everyone who had laughed at him that spring for what he'd refused to do.

Torvald was a proud man, though not an unkind one, which is a distinction worth making because pride alone rarely ruins a man — it is pride joined to good luck that does the real damage, since good luck teaches pride that it was right all along. He ran the largest flock in the northern reach of the valley, larger than his father's had been, larger than any of his neighbors', and he had built it stone by stone, lamb by lamb, through weather that had thinned other men's herds to nothing. He was not wrong to be proud of that. He had simply come to believe that the flock's size was proof of something about him personally, rather than proof that the mountain had, so far, been generous to him in particular.

It was old Ossian — this was well before his final winters, when he still walked the valley with his stick and his opinions — who first put the idea to the households at the spring gathering. He proposed that every flock-owning family in the valley, great or small, should set aside each year a small toll: a tenth-part of the wool clip, or its worth in lambs for those years the clip ran thin, to be kept in the long stone barn at the valley's center, under the joint key of three chosen keepers, myself among them from the second year onward. The wool and lambs would sit there, growing neither larger nor smaller through anyone's private wanting, until such time as a slide or a plague or a hard flood took a household's flock entire, at which point that household would be made whole again out of the common store — not made rich, mind you, only made whole, restored to where they had stood the week before disaster found them.

"And what," said Torvald, standing at the back of the gathering with his arms crossed the way a man crosses them when he has already decided, "do I get for my tenth-part, if the mountain never troubles me?"

"You get," said Ossian, "the mountain never troubling you."

There was some laughter at this, not unkind, but Torvald did not laugh, and he did not pay his tenth-part that year, nor the next three after it. He said, and said it reasonably enough that some men nodded along, that he had built his flock through his own care and his own weather-sense, rising before dawn to read the sky, choosing his high pastures with more caution than his neighbors chose theirs, and he did not see why he should hand over good wool to cover the losses of men who grazed carelessly on unsound ground or failed to watch their folds for the early signs of rot. Let each man's flock answer for that man's judgment, he said. That was only fair.

It is worth saying plainly that he was not entirely wrong about the fairness of it, in the narrow sense he meant. Some households did graze more carelessly than his. But he had mistaken a narrow truth for the whole of the matter, the way a man standing in a doorway mistakes the room behind him for the whole of the house.

The families who did pay found the barn's reserve called upon twice in those years — once for the Aldric household, whose fold sickened with a foot-rot that took forty ewes before it was checked, and once for a widow named Sable Karrow, whose entire flock, all thirty head, drowned in a flash flood off the eastern scree while she was down in the lower valley selling wool. Both households were made whole from the common barn within the season, the flocks restocked from the pooled lambs and the wool credited against what they owed the traders, and both households went on much as before, a little shaken but not ruined. Torvald observed this and said nothing, which for a proud man is its own kind of speech.

Then came the year of the slide.

It was a wet spring that year, wetter than any in memory, and the high slope above Torvald's summer pasture — a slope he had grazed for eleven years without incident, reading it each season as carefully as he read the sky — let go all at once on an afternoon in the third week after shearing. There was no warning worth the name; a groan in the earth, Fen told me later, having heard it from a cousin who'd been herding nearby, and then the whole green shoulder of the mountain came down as a single moving thing, and when it stopped moving a hundred and eighty of Torvald's two hundred sheep were under it, along with two of his dogs, and Torvald himself was left standing at the pasture's edge with twenty sheep and the particular stillness of a man watching his life's accounting rewritten in under a minute.

He did not come to the valley center for three days. When he did come, he came to the tally-house, not the common barn, and he asked me — I was keeper that year — what he owed in back-toll if he wished to draw on the reserve, since he had paid nothing in four years and felt, he said, that he had no right to ask.

I told him what Ossian had told the gathering long before: that the arrangement was not a ledger of exact debts repaid with exact interest, precisely because no man could know in advance whether he would be the one paying in for thirty years and drawing nothing, or paying in for one year and drawing everything. That was the whole of its use. A man who waited to join until he could calculate his advantage had already missed the reason it existed. I told him the barn's keepers would restock him regardless, because that was what the barn was for, but that going forward he would be expected to pay his tenth-part like any other household, including some years of back-toll to settle the account with his own conscience if not with ours.

He paid it. He paid it every year after, without complaint and, I think, eventually without resentment, though it took him some seasons to say so aloud. What he said to me, the one time he did speak of it plainly, was that he had spent eleven years believing his flock's safety was a thing he had built with his own hands out of his own good judgment, and had needed one afternoon to learn that his hands and his judgment had only ever been standing on the same mountain as everyone else's, and the mountain did not consult a man's pride before it decided where to slide.

A household's ruin from flood, slide, or plague strikes without regard for merit or carefulness, and no single flock, however well-tended, can absorb a loss large enough to end it. When many households each set aside a small, steady share into a common reserve, the rare disaster that would destroy one alone is instead spread thin enough across all to be borne by none too heavily — and the toll paid in quiet years is not wasted, but is the very price of not standing alone in the bad one.

SEVENTEEN — The Fashionable Fleece

I watched my neighbor pay four hundred dollars for a Beanie Baby in 1998. A stuffed bear. Purple, if I remember right. She was convinced—absolutely certain—that it would fund her daughter's college tuition in ten years. She'd done the math, she said. Checked the price guides. Joined the collector forums.

I ran into her at a yard sale six years later. The bear was in a cardboard box marked "Free." She didn't want to talk about it.

That image stuck with me longer than it should have, because I've done the same thing. Different asset, same fever.

In the valley where I grew up, the obsession was smoke-fleece. That's not a metaphor I'm stretching to make a point—it's what we actually called it. A rare genetic mutation that turned a ram's wool the color of storm clouds. Beautiful, yes. Useful? Not particularly. No warmer, no more durable, no easier to work with. Just rare.

Tomas Aldric's ram produced it first. I remember the morning he brought the lamb to market—traders showed up before sunrise, which never happened. They bid against each other in whispers, the way people do when they're trying to hide how badly they want something. The final price got passed around the valley for weeks, growing a little each time someone retold it.

Within a season, half the shepherds I knew were breeding for smoke-fleece. Selling off their reliable stock—sheep that had fed their families for generations—to buy breeding pairs that carried the trait. The math was simple, they said. If one ram fetched that price, imagine what a whole flock could bring.

Cael was Fen's cousin. (Fen's the one I mentioned earlier—steady, careful, the kind of shepherd who checks his fences twice.) Cael sold off two-thirds of his working flock and sank everything into smoke-fleece breeding stock. I remember him at the shearing fair that year, walking like he'd already won something. He had this way of standing that made you feel like you'd missed an opportunity he'd been smart enough to seize.

I wanted to be him. That's the part I'm supposed to gloss over in a chapter about the dangers of chasing trends, but it's true. I looked at my own mixed flock—browns, creams, the occasional white—and felt embarrassed. Fen caught me pricing breeding stock one afternoon and just raised an eyebrow. Didn't say anything. Didn't need to.

The thing about trends is they don't announce themselves as trends while they're happening. They feel like the future. They feel like the smart money finally figuring out what something is really worth. You're not speculating—you're correcting an inefficiency everyone else was too slow to notice.

Idris Vane didn't correct anything. She was a widow who'd inherited her flock from her husband, and she ran it the same way he had, the same way his father had. At that same shearing fair where Cael was strutting, traders walked past her stock without slowing down. One of them actually laughed—I heard him—said something about "commodity wool" like it was an insult.

Idris shrugged. She'd heard worse.

By year three, people who'd never owned a sheep in their lives were buying breeding stock. The prices kept climbing because everyone was buying to breed, not to shear. The market was farmers selling to farmers selling to farmers, all of them betting the music wouldn't stop.

It stopped.

Some fashion house in the southern cities decided smoke-fleece was last season. They wanted ivory now, or maybe it was charcoal—I don't remember. It doesn't matter. What matters is the traders stopped coming. The breeding stock everyone had paid double for was suddenly worth half what a working ram cost. Less, because by then they'd been bred for color instead of hardiness, and half of them couldn't handle a cold winter.

Cael lost his farm. Not immediately—it took three years of trying to rebuild what he'd had before, taking on debt to replace the flock he'd sold off, falling behind on the interest. But it started the day the smoke-fleece market collapsed. I remember seeing him at the auction when they sold off his land. He didn't look angry. He looked confused, like he was still trying to figure out which step he'd gotten wrong.

I should tell you that I learned from watching him, that I stuck with my mixed flock and felt vindicated.

I didn't. I chased something else two years later—a "tax-advantaged" investment scheme that a very convincing man explained to me over drinks. It wasn't sheep, but it was the same fever. The same certainty that I'd found the edge everyone else had missed. I got out before it collapsed completely, but only because I got lucky with timing, not because I'd gotten smarter.

That's the hardest part to admit: watching Cael lose everything didn't inoculate me. I still wanted to believe the next thing would be different.

Idris, meanwhile, kept shearing her flock every spring. The wool sold for average prices—sometimes a little above, sometimes a little below, depending on the year. Over a decade, it averaged out to steady. Not spectacular. Not exciting. But steady.

She bought a new barn with her savings. Sent her daughter to trade school. Retired at sixty-eight with enough to live on. None of that makes for a dramatic story, which is maybe why people don't tell it.

Here's what I wish someone had told me, in language blunt enough that I couldn't ignore it: the cost of chasing trends isn't the money you lose when they collapse. It's the decade you spend recovering. It's the compounding you miss while you're clawing back to zero. It's the night you lie awake at fifty-seven doing math on how many more years you'll need to work, and realizing the answer is "more than you have left."

Cael was forty-three when he lost the farm. He's sixty now. Still working. He'll die working, most likely.

The returns you miss matter more than the losses you take. That's not intuitive, but it's true. If you're thirty and you chase three trends that fail, you might break even on the money—win one, lose two, end up roughly where you started. But you're not where you started. You're forty with fifteen years of missed compounding behind you, and no amount of spectacular returns in your fifties will close that gap.

So here's the actionable part, the thing you can do Monday morning:

Go look at your investment accounts—all of them. Not to check performance. To check how many times you've moved money in the last three years. Every time you sold one position to chase another, write down the date and what you were chasing. If there are more than three entries, you're not investing. You're speculating. And speculation has a perfect long-term track record: it transfers money from people who do it to people who don't.

If that feels too harsh, if you want to argue that some of those moves were smart, that you were responding to real information—fine. Track it. Write down what you expect each current position to do in the next five years. Specific numbers. Then put the paper somewhere you'll find it in five years and see if you were right.

Most people won't do this because most people already know what they'll find.

I still have that piece of paper from my own version of this exercise. I was wrong about seven out of nine positions. The two I got right were the ones I'd held longest and thought about least. The ones I'd almost forgotten I owned.

That's not a feel-good lesson about patience winning. It's a mechanical fact about how markets work: the longer you hold something broadly sound, the more ways you have to be right. The shorter you hold it, the more ways you have to be wrong.

Idris didn't know that in theory. She just knew her flock worked. She knew the wool sold. She knew if she kept doing what worked, she'd be fine. And she was right, but not because she was lucky. She was right because "keep doing what works" is the only strategy that survives contact with a decade of random trends.

Cael knew more than she did. He'd read the market reports. Studied the genetics. Talked to the traders. He had information. It didn't save him. Information about what's fashionable right now is just expensive gossip.

The question isn't whether the next trend will pay off. Some will. The question is whether you'll know which ones in advance, consistently, better than the crowd. And if you're honest—if you look at your own track record, not the story you tell yourself about your track record—the answer is almost certainly no.

I didn't want to write this chapter. I wanted to write the one where I figured out the pattern, got smart, stopped chasing. But that's not what happened. I still feel the pull every time something new catches fire. I just don't act on it anymore, and some days that feels less like wisdom and more like being too tired to make another mistake.

Maybe that's what getting older is. You don't stop wanting the shortcut. You just run out of time to recover from taking it.

EIGHTEEN — The Overgrazed Slope

There is a shelf of pasture above the valley where the mountain flattens itself out for a while before climbing again. The old ones called it the High Common, though it had no fence and no gate—only a line of white stones set into the ground by hands so long dead that no one living had known them.

I have walked that line myself, counting stones the way I count tally-marks. I can tell you it took a patient people to lay it. Patient, and afraid of the alternative, though they never said so aloud in any story that reached me.

The custom was this: each household with grazing rights to the Common could put up so many sheep to it for the short high-summer weeks, and no more. The number was reckoned by the size of a family's home-pasture below, so that no one carried more of the mountain's grass away than they had put good grass into keeping through the rest of the year. It was not written on paper. It did not need to be. Ossian, when he was still a young man and not yet the white-bearded fixture I knew, used to say that the Common kept its own ledger in the color of its grass, and that anyone who wanted to cheat it was cheating a thing that remembered.

For three generations, by the reckoning of the tally-sticks kept in the valley chest, the Common held. Families grazed it in the short weeks of true summer, brought their flocks down before the grass thinned past its own recovering, and the shelf greened again every spring as it always had—thick and short and sweet, the kind of grass that makes wool grow dense.

Then it began, as these things do, without any single villain and without any single day you could put your finger on and say: here is where it broke.

There was a household—the Ambrose family, three brothers who had inherited their father's flock all at once and split it three ways. Each brother wanted his own third to look as prosperous as the whole had once looked. One summer, finding their home-pasture crowded with the three flocks fighting over one man's worth of grass, they sent an extra dozen ewes up to the Common beyond their customary count.

A dozen sheep. On a shelf that fed perhaps four hundred.

Who would notice a dozen more mouths in among so much green?

No one did notice. Or if they noticed, no one said anything, because it is an uncomfortable thing to walk up to your neighbor and accuse him of counting wrong. Easier by far to tell yourself it was an honest error, or a hard year, or none of your business. Easier to look at your own flock and keep your mouth shut.

The next summer the Ambrose brothers sent the same dozen extra, now grown into the custom of it. And a family named Hurst, who had watched them do it unremarked the year before, reasoned that if the Ambrose flock could graze past the line and take no harm from it, then a family with five children to clothe and no reputation for wealth to protect might be forgiven a little excess too.

So the Hursts added six ewes past their count.

And a third family, seeing both of these go unpunished, thought: someone is already grazing past the limit; if I hold to my old number while they take the extra grass, I am the fool of the valley, feeding the Common's bounty into my neighbor's wool and getting nothing for my restraint. Better to take my share of what is apparently there for the taking, before it is gone.

You might be thinking this sounds like simple greed, and I should tell you now to guard yourself against it, to be better than the Ambrose brothers, to hold the line when others won't—though I should say I have never once held a line like that when I thought no one was watching and the cost of breaking it seemed small enough to slip past unnoticed. I can tell you what you should do. I cannot tell you I have done it.

What I can tell you is this: no one climbed the mountain that summer meaning to ruin it.

That is the part I want you to hear plainly, because it is the part that does the damage and the part that is hardest to see while it is happening. Each household reasoned only about its own dozen sheep, its own six ewes, its own small and private math, and each household's math was, taken alone, perfectly sound. A dozen sheep is nothing to a shelf of pasture that size.

But a dozen sheep from three households is thirty-six. Thirty-six from five is sixty. And by the fourth summer of this slow creeping—I have this from the tally-sticks, which recorded flock numbers even when they recorded nothing of grazing weeks—there were perhaps two hundred more sheep on the High Common in the hardest weeks of summer than the shelf had ever been asked to carry.

The grass did not vanish all at once. That is not how a pasture dies.

It thinned first, in patches, near the water troughs where the flocks gathered most. The old-timers who walked up to check on it said the same thing Ossian's father was said to have said in a much earlier bad year: the Common is looking tired. But tired grass still looks like grass from a distance. And the summer was good. And the wool came down heavy that autumn, heavier than it had in years, because of course it did—more sheep on the mountain meant more wool in the sacks.

No one wanted to be the one to ask whether the heaviness would last.

It did not last.

By the fifth summer the shelf that had once gone knee-high and thick by the solstice was cropped down to bristle by midsummer. The roots chewed so short and so often that they had no time between grazings to send anything back up. Where the roots gave out entirely—near the troughs and along the worn paths—the bare ground showed through like scalp through thinning hair. When the autumn rains came they did not sink in the way rain should sink into good turf. They ran. They carried the thin soil with them down the gullies and left stone showing in bands where grass had held for longer than any living person could remember.

I want you to imagine what that fifth autumn felt like, not for the valley as a whole but for one family in it. Say you are the Hursts, the ones who added six ewes past your count because the Ambrose brothers had gone unpunished and you reasoned that you would be a fool to hold back while they profited. You brought your flock down from the Common that autumn and your wool sacks were lighter than they had been in four years. Not because your own six extra ewes had somehow eaten less. They had not. They had eaten their fill, same as always. But the Common itself was failing, and when a pasture fails it does not ask whose sheep did the worst of the damage. It fails for everyone together.

You stood in your wool shed that autumn and looked at the thin sacks and thought about the years before, when the wool had come down heavy, and you thought: I should have taken more then, when there was more to be taken. If I had known the good years would not last, I would have sent eight ewes instead of six, or ten, or twelve. I held back just enough to feel virtuous and not enough to make any difference. I got the worst of both—the guilt of cheating and the poverty of restraint.

That is what the cost feels like from the inside. Not wicked. Not foolish, even. Just late. Always a step behind the people who reasoned faster than you did, and a step ahead of the people who reasoned slower, and all of you arriving at the same empty place together, blaming each other for thinking the same thought at different speeds.

That was the year old Ossian—not yet old, but getting there, a man in his stern middle years with a voice that carried across a sheep pen without effort—called every household with a right to the Common down to the valley floor on a single evening. He did not shout. Shouting was not his way. He laid the tally-sticks for five years running out on a plank table so that anyone could walk along them and see the numbers climb, household by household, name by name.

I am told the Ambrose brothers went red and then pale. The Hursts said nothing at all. Others who had told themselves quietly that everyone surely does it now sat with their hands in their laps and could not meet the eyes across the table, because the sticks did not lie and did not care whose feelings the truth inconvenienced.

There was no single culprit to punish, which made it a harder evening than a simple theft would have made it. Ossian did not try to make it simple. What he did instead was propose a thing that had never been needed before: a common keeper for the Common. A person—and for some years it was Ossian himself, and later it fell to others—whose whole task was to walk the shelf before the season and set the summer's true carrying number based on what the grass could bear that year, not what any household wished it could bear, and to count the flocks going up and coming down, publicly, at the white stones, so that no dozen extra ewes could climb unremarked again.

The recovery took the better part of six years. Six years of grazing the Common lighter than even the old customary number, resting sections of it in rotation, watching the bare scalp-patches fight their way back to turf a hand's width at a time. Wool was thinner from every flock in those years. More than one household grumbled that the cure seemed harsher than the disease, forgetting, as people do, that the disease had been of their own slow making and had cost them the very abundance they were now missing.

I think of the Ambrose brothers sometimes, not unkindly. They were not wicked men. Only men doing sums that stopped at the border of their own flock, the way most of us do most of our sums. Each one of them could have told you, and told you truly, that his dozen ewes changed nothing. They were right, each one taken alone.

It was only all of them together, unwatched and unadmitted, that changed everything.

Here is what I wish someone had told the Hursts, or the Ambrose brothers, or any of the families who climbed that mountain with their dozen extra sheep and their perfectly sound reasoning: You cannot out-optimize a system that depends on everyone not optimizing. And you cannot know, ahead of time, whether you are living inside such a system or not, because the systems that collapse from private reasoning always look like they are holding right up until the summer they are not.

The common keeper was not a perfect solution. He had to be paid, which meant every household gave up a portion of their wool to fund him. He made mistakes. Some years he set the number too low and families left wool on the mountain that might have been shorn. Other years he set it too high and the grass came back thinner than it should have. But what he gave them, in exchange for the imperfection and the cost, was a chance to stop thinking about whether their neighbor was grazing one more ewe than his pasture had earned him. He let them look at their own flocks and know that the count going up the mountain was a count the grass could hold, not because every household had chosen to be good that year, but because someone had been paid to make goodness irrelevant to the outcome.

I do not know if your life has a High Common in it. I do not know what your dozen extra sheep look like, or whether you have already sent them up the mountain, or whether you are still standing at the white stones trying to decide if anyone would notice.

What I know is this: if you are doing math on a shared system and your math stops at the edge of your own benefit, you are reasoning the way the Ambrose brothers reasoned, and the Hursts, and every family that looked at the Common and thought a little more won't be noticed. Your math may be sound. It probably is. That is not the question.

The question is whether the system you are inside can survive everyone doing sound math at the same time.

And if the answer is no, or if you do not know the answer, then the next question is not whether you should be better or stronger or less selfish than you are. The next question is whether you are willing to pay someone—some structure, some council, some outside counter you did not choose and do not control—to stop you from having to choose goodness every time the grass looks thick enough to take a little more.

I have spent enough years on this to tell you: it is easier to live with a keeper you resent than with a Common you ruined because you trusted yourself to hold a line no one was counting.

But I have also spent enough years on this to know that the hardest part is not agreeing to the keeper. The hardest part is the evening when the tally-sticks come out and you see your own name written there among the others, and you have to sit at the table and admit you were one of the ones who climbed past the stones when you thought no one would notice.

That evening is coming for you, or it has already come, or you are sitting in it now and pretending it is someone else's count on the sticks.

I cannot tell you what to do with that. I can only tell you that the families who stayed in the valley, the ones whose flocks are still grazing the Common now, decades after the thin years—those were the families who sat through that evening and did not leave the table. They paid for the keeper. They grazed lighter. They watched the grass come back a hand's width at a time and did not ask to be forgiven for the years when they had grazed it down.

The question I have been walking toward, the one I did not know I was walking toward when I started telling you about the white stones and the Ambrose brothers, is not whether you can be trusted to hold the line.

The question is whether you are willing to be counted.

NINETEEN — The Handshake at the Ford

Cold air came down off the pass before the sun did, most mornings, and it was on such a morning — thin light, the grass still hard with frost — that I first heard the name Bevan Ostler, though I did not know then how long I would go on hearing it.

I was a girl, still keeping my mother's flock more than my own, and I had walked down to the ford to fill the water skins because the well nearer the house had gone brackish that autumn. The ford was where our valley's cart track crossed the river before climbing out toward the lowland roads, and it was there, more than any other place, that the valley met the outside world. Wool traders coming up in late summer with their mule trains. Salt sellers. The occasional tinker with his cart of bent nails and promises.

Most transactions of any size in those days were done at the ford, in the open, with the water running past as a kind of witness that couldn't be bribed or made to forget.

That morning there were two men standing in the shallows arguing about a ram.

One was Tobin Ashgrove, a shepherd from the upper meadows whose family I knew the way you know everyone in a small valley, which is to say completely and yet not well at all. The other was the wool trader, Bevan Ostler — a broad, weathered man who came up from the lowlands twice a year with his mules and his ledger book, though I never once saw him consult the ledger for anything that mattered. What mattered, for Ostler, lived in his memory and in his handshake. This was widely understood to be more reliable than most men's paper.

The argument, such as it was, concerned a ram Tobin wanted. A big-boned grey animal with good conformation that Ostler had brought up from a breeder in the south, meaning to sell it along the way for a fair price to whoever wanted new blood in their flock. Tobin wanted it badly. His own ram had died of a bloat that spring and his ewes were coming into their cycle with no sire worth the name.

A season lost breeding is not a small thing when you live by wool and lambs.

But Tobin did not have the money. Not then. He had spent what savings he had rebuilding a wall the winter had knocked down, and wool money wouldn't come in until shearing, months off.

I stood at the water's edge with my skins half full and listened, the way children do, without seeming to.

"I'll pay you at shearing," Tobin said. "Full price, plus what's fair for waiting."

Ostler looked at him for a long moment. He was not a sentimental man, whatever else he was, and traders who extend credit on nothing but a face and a name do not stay traders for long, as a rule. But he had dealt with Tobin's father before him. Knew the family bred true — not the sheep, the people.

"Full price," Ostler said, "plus a fifth over, for the waiting and the risk. Here, at this ford, come shearing. I'll be through in six weeks on my way back down, and I'll collect it then."

"Here at the ford," Tobin agreed.

And they shook on it. In the cold water. Nothing written down anywhere, because there was no notary within four days' ride and even if there had been, neither man would have thought to trouble one. The ram changed hands. Tobin led it up the track toward his meadows, well pleased, and Ostler went on about his rounds, and I finished filling my skins and thought no more of it, being a child, and children do not yet understand what a spoken promise costs to keep.

I did not think of it again, in fact, for six weeks.

Until the day Ostler came back through, as he'd said he would, and stood once more at the ford, waiting.

Here is what I should tell you about those six weeks, though to be honest I didn't understand any of this until years later when my mother filled in what I'd missed as a child: disaster had found Tobin's flock the way it finds most shepherds sooner or later, without asking permission or picking a convenient season. A sickness had gone through his ewes in the last fortnight before shearing — not a plague that killed outright, but a wasting thing that soured their fleece and left half his flock too weak to shear properly. What wool he brought to market that year was thin and poor and fetched barely half what he'd counted on.

He had, in addition, three ewes dead outright. A debt to a neighbor for medicine that hadn't worked in any case. And a ram he could not afford standing in his fold, eating his hay, while the man he owed was already on the road back to collect.

My mother told me the whole valley knew Tobin was ruined that season, or near enough to it. She said people talked about it the way they talked about weather — matter-of-factly, with the kind of sympathy that doesn't cost anything because everyone knew there was nothing to be done. A man cannot pay what he does not have.

Ostler, everyone assumed, would simply write off the ram as a loss and be more careful with his credit next time, as traders learn to be.

No one would have blamed Tobin much for failing to show up at the ford.

And this is the part I want you to sit with for a moment, because it matters more than what came after: there was a version of that day where Tobin simply did not go down to the water. Where he stayed in his upper meadow and let the hour pass and told himself — and he would have been right, by any reasonable measure — that a man who has lost half his flock to sickness and has three dead ewes and a ruined shearing cannot be expected to make good on a debt given in better times.

He could have sent word later, through someone else, that he'd pay what he could when he could, and Ostler would have accepted it or not, and either way the matter would have faded into the general blur of hardship and compromise that makes up most of any shepherd's life.

I have seen this happen. Not once. Dozens of times. A promise made in good faith, eroded by circumstance until the promising itself seems like a kind of innocent mistake, something that belonged to a more optimistic season and has no business surviving into the present. And the thing is, it does not even feel like breaking your word when you do it. It feels like being realistic. It feels like adapting. It feels, above all, like the only thing a reasonable person could do under the circumstances.

The cost of that reasonableness is not visible in the moment. It does not announce itself.

It happens later, quietly, in the form of your own name becoming less valuable. In traders who used to stop at your fold now riding past it because they have heard you are the sort of man whose word holds only when it's convenient. In neighbors who do not offer you the ewe you need on credit next spring because they remember that credit, in your hands, becomes negotiable. In your own son, years on, discovering that the market will not take his handshake seriously because his father taught the valley that handshakes, in your family, are conditional.

You do not lose one transaction. You lose the capacity to transact.

And here is what no one tells you about that kind of loss: it is nearly impossible to rebuild. You cannot wake up one morning and decide to be trustworthy again. You cannot make a single good decision and have it erase the pattern. Trust, in a valley with no magistrate to enforce a contract, is the only currency that matters, and once you have spent it, you are trading with nothing.

But when Ostler came down the track that evening and stood again at the water, Tobin was there waiting for him.

And he had the money.

Not all of it in coin — my mother was clear on this point, because it became something people told each other for years afterward, the way a valley keeps its stories. He had sold two of his own ewes, the strongest ones left to him, animals he could not spare and that any sensible man would have kept back to rebuild his flock. He had sold a good copper kettle that had been his mother's. He had taken on a debt to old Ossian, who was not old yet then but was already the sort of man people went to when they needed patience more than money.

And he stood at the ford in the last light with the full sum — the fifth over included — and put it in Ostler's hand.

"You didn't need to make yourself whole on my account," Ostler said, or so the story runs, and I have heard it told with small variations my whole life, which is how you know a story has been handled by many hands and is still true in its bones. "I'd have carried you another season. Any man could see what happened to your flock wasn't your doing."

"You didn't ask what happened to my flock when you gave me the ram," Tobin said. "You asked would I pay you at the ford. I said I would."

That was the whole of it, as near as anyone remembers the words.

He did not make a speech of it. He was not, by every account, an especially eloquent man, and I think this matters, because the ones who make a speech of their own honesty are usually selling something. Tobin simply believed that a thing said at a crossing, in front of running water, with another man's hand in his, was not a thing that circumstance got to unmake later.

The circumstance was his to suffer. The promise was not his to break, whatever it cost him to keep it.

Now I should say — because I have spent the last several paragraphs making Tobin sound like a moral exemplar, and that was not quite what he was — that the decision to sell those ewes nearly broke his wife's heart, and that the debt to Ossian took him three years to clear, and that there were nights, I am told, when he sat by his own fire and wondered if he had been a fool. Wondered if Ostler would have even remembered the debt six months on, let alone held him to it. Wondered if he had traded his family's security for the sake of something as insubstantial as a reputation.

I don't know what he concluded on those nights. My mother did not tell me that part, and I never knew Tobin well enough myself to ask.

But I do know this: Ostler kept coming to our valley for another twenty years after that, long past the point where he needed to bother with a place so small and hard to reach, and when I once asked him why — I was grown by then, and kept the tally-stones, and traders spoke more freely to the keeper of the stones than to most — he said something I never forgot.

He said he had traded in a hundred valleys and market towns in his life, some with courts and contracts and men paid to enforce them, and none of it, he said, was worth as much as a handshake at our ford.

Because paper only tells a man what he is required to do.

It never once told him what kind of man he was.

Tobin rebuilt his flock over the following years. Slowly, the way these things go. He was never what you'd call a wealthy man — the sale of those two ewes set him back in ways that compounded, season after season, because a smaller flock means less wool and fewer lambs and less capacity to weather the next bad winter. Optimization, if you are keeping score, would tell you he made the wrong call. That he should have kept the ewes, broken the promise, preserved his capital.

But he was a man whose word other traders sought out for the rest of his life, and that, in a valley with no law but each other, was the nearer thing to wealth.

I think about Tobin when I am tempted to renegotiate a commitment I made in a more optimistic season. When the terms I agreed to six months ago feel unreasonable now because my circumstances have changed, or the market has shifted, or I have simply learned something new that makes my old promise inconvenient. The voice that says *be realistic* is loud, and it is almost always correct about the facts. The facts are that I cannot afford this. That no one would blame me. That the other party will understand.

What that voice does not tell me is that I am not merely deciding whether to keep this one promise.

I am deciding what my name will mean the next time I say it at a crossing.

TWENTY — The Flock Passed Down

I was forty-three years old when I realized I'd been thinking about inheritance completely wrong.

Standing in my father's workshop—he'd already been gone two years by then—I found myself holding a ledger he'd kept from 1987 to 2003. Sixteen years of careful notes about which investments he'd made, which ones tanked, what he'd learned. I'd inherited his accounts, sure. But I'd never seen this ledger while he was alive. Never watched him make a single decision. Never asked why he sold that rental property in '92 or why he kept those municipal bonds through the '94 rate spike.

I had his money. I didn't have his judgment.

That's when I started thinking about Old Faron.

Faron was a real shepherd—lived three valleys over from where I grew up in northern Wales, died in 2001 at seventy-nine. My mother knew his wife through the wool cooperative. What made Faron different wasn't the size of his flock, though it was impressive—over two hundred breeding ewes by the time he was sixty. What made him different was what he did at sixty-one.

He gave forty of those ewes to his son Torvald outright. Not when he died. While he was still healthy enough to watch what happened next.

Torvald was twenty-six. He'd worked alongside his father since he was old enough to carry a bucket, but he'd never made a consequential decision on his own. Faron handed him those forty ewes and said—this is how Torvald told it at the pub years later—"They're yours. You decide which ones to breed, which to sell, when to move them to winter pasture. I'll watch. I won't fix your mistakes unless you're about to kill something."

That first year, Torvald lost eleven ewes. He moved them to pasture too early, before the ground had dried, and foot rot spread through the flock. Faron watched it happen. Didn't intervene until Torvald came to him, exhausted, asking what he was doing wrong.

"You're learning," Faron said. "Expensive learning, but it won't kill you. Fix it now, and you'll never make that mistake with two hundred."

Most fathers I knew—most people I knew, honestly—took the opposite approach. Build the estate as large as possible, protect it carefully, hand it over intact when you die. Let your kids figure it out then. Torvald's cousin Peit inherited that way. His father Brannoc died suddenly at fifty-seven—heart attack while mending a fence—and Peit, twenty-four and utterly unprepared, found himself responsible for three hundred ewes, two pastures, and debts he didn't know existed.

Peit sold half the flock within eighteen months just to stay solvent. Not because he was stupid or lazy. Because he'd never been allowed to make a decision that mattered while someone was still around to explain what he'd done wrong.

I should say—though I'm probably the last person who should be giving advice about this—that the conventional approach isn't entirely wrong. There's something to be said for preserving wealth, for not letting your kids blow through your life's work while you're still alive to watch. I've seen that happen too. My uncle gave my cousin Danny forty thousand pounds when Danny was thirty, meant to be seed capital for a business. Danny bought a boat. Not a fishing boat. A pleasure yacht. Sold it two years later for half what he paid.

But here's what I actually did with my own daughter, and I'm still not sure it was the right call: When she was twenty-eight and working her first real job—project manager at a tech consultancy—I opened a brokerage account in her name and put in twenty thousand pounds. Not as a gift. As a teaching exercise.

"This is real money," I told her. "You can invest it however you want. You keep any gains. You eat any losses. I'll answer questions, but I won't tell you what to buy."

She lost £2,400 in the first six months buying individual stocks she'd read about on Reddit. Mostly companies she didn't understand—crypto-adjacent things, SPACs, a cannabis company that went bankrupt. I watched it happen. It was physically painful not to step in.

Then she called me, frustrated, asking why everything she touched seemed to lose money. That's when we had the conversation about index funds, diversification, why exciting stories rarely translate to good returns. She restructured the account. It's worth £31,000 now, four years later. More importantly, she knows why.

When I die—and I hope that's not for another thirty years, but you never know—she'll inherit whatever I've managed not to spend. Could be a decent amount. Could be less than I hope. But she'll inherit it knowing what a market correction feels like, what it's like to see red numbers on a screen and have to decide whether to sell or hold, what happens when you chase performance.

She'll have judgment. Not just money.

That's what Faron understood. By the time he died, Torvald had been managing his own flock—grown from forty ewes to ninety—for thirteen years. He'd been through two bad winters, a wool price collapse, a parasite outbreak. He'd made mistakes Faron could watch and correct. When Faron finally passed, Torvald inherited the remaining flock, but the transition was barely noticeable. He already knew how to do everything. He'd already done it.

The alternative—Peit's inheritance—looked more generous on paper. Three hundred ewes versus Torvald's forty. But Peit spent the next decade struggling, selling off assets, learning through catastrophic mistakes instead of manageable ones. Last I heard, he'd left farming entirely. Works in construction now in Bangor.

You might be thinking this only applies if you've got wealth to pass down. I thought that too. But I was wrong—or at least I was thinking about it too narrowly.

My father worked in a factory his entire adult life. Died with maybe £40,000 in savings and a paid-off house. Not nothing, but not wealth by most definitions. What he should have passed down—what I wish he'd passed down—wasn't money. It was the logic behind the decisions he made.

Why he always kept six months of expenses in cash even when it earned nothing. Why he never financed a car. Why he put money into Premium Bonds instead of chasing higher returns. I didn't learn any of that until after he died and I found that ledger.

I had to reverse-engineer his thinking from old notebooks. It would have been so much easier if he'd just shown me while he was alive. If he'd said, "Here's what I'm thinking about this decision, here's what I'm worried about, here's what I've learned from the last time I tried something like this."

The cost of not doing this—and I've felt this cost, so I know it's real—is that your kids spend their first decade of adult financial life making mistakes you already made. Mistakes you could have helped them avoid, or at least helped them make smaller and less devastating.

I watched my daughter lose that £2,400 and it hurt. But it would have hurt so much more to watch her lose £24,000 at forty-five because she'd never learned the lesson.

Here's what you can actually do with this, and I mean tomorrow, not someday:

If you have adult children—and I mean actually adult, mid-twenties or older—have a real conversation with them about a financial decision you're making right now. Not a lecture. A real conversation. "I'm thinking about refinancing the mortgage, here's why, here's what I'm worried about, what do you think?" Let them see you think through it. Let them see you be uncertain. Let them see you make the choice and, six months later, whether it worked out.

If you don't have kids but you have younger siblings, nieces, nephews, mentees—same thing. Find someone a generation behind you and let them watch you make a real decision. Explain your reasoning. Tell them what you're afraid of getting wrong.

If you're the younger generation and your parents are still alive—and this is harder, I know, because it requires them to be willing—ask them about a decision they're making. Not their whole financial life, that's too big and too intrusive. One decision. "Dad, I noticed you sold those bonds, can I ask why?" See if they'll let you in.

The point isn't to be perfect. The point is to let the people who come after you see how you think, while you're still around to explain it.

Torvald told me once—this was at Faron's funeral, actually—that the most valuable thing his father gave him wasn't the flock. It was the running commentary. Every time they walked the pastures together, Faron would narrate his thinking. "See that ewe limping? We'll watch her for three days. If she's not better, we'll check for foot rot. If it's foot rot, we separate her immediately. If it's a stone bruise, it'll heal on its own."

Small things. Constant repetition. By the time Torvald was thirty, he could think like his father without his father being there.

That's what I'm trying to build now with my daughter. Not a pile of money—though I hope to leave her some. A way of thinking about money that won't make her afraid of it. That's the actual inheritance that matters.

Because the real goal here—and I think this is what Faron understood at sixty-one when he gave away those forty ewes—isn't to die with the biggest estate. It's to stop being afraid of money early enough that you can enjoy whatever years you have left, and to pass down that fearlessness to whoever comes next.

I still have my father's ledger. I've started keeping one of my own, and I've told my daughter where it is. Not for after I die. For now. She can read it whenever she wants. See what I'm thinking, what I'm worried about, what I got wrong last year.

Small stakes now, while I'm here to explain. That's the inheritance worth giving.

TWENTY-ONE — The Second Trade

There was a year the wool trade fell out of the world, or so it seemed to us up in the high fold, though I have since learned it fell only out of the towns below, where the traders and the weavers and the men with ledgers decided among themselves that wool was worth half what it had been the season before, and no one troubled to send us word until the buyers came up the pass in autumn and offered prices that made old men laugh out loud, not from mirth.

I was younger then, keeper only of the small tallies, not yet of the whole valley's memory, and I watched it happen to two households that had grazed within a stone's throw of each other my whole life, the Ambrose family and the Tull family, and if you had asked me before that year which of them stood the sturdier, I could not have told you, for both kept good flocks and good order and neither drank away their earnings nor let their fences rot.

Aldous Ambrose ran perhaps the finest sheep in that end of the valley. He had an eye for a ewe the way some men have an eye for weather, and he had built his flock over twenty years into something other shepherds walked a mile out of their way to admire. But Aldous held to one article of faith above all others, which was that a shepherd's whole business was sheep, and that anything else a man turned his hand to was a kind of infidelity to the flock, a wandering of attention that the animals would somehow sense and suffer for. His wife Ivet had once, years before, taken up carding and spinning in the winter months, selling small skeins to travelers who passed through for the high pastures in summer, and Aldous had let her keep at it so long as it amused her, but he never counted it as anything, never wrote it in his book, called it her thread money as though it were a kind of pocket change unworthy of the household ledger. Every coin that mattered in that house, every debt paid and every roof mended and every daughter's dowry saved toward, came from the wool clip and nothing else. When the price fell that autumn, it did not merely dent the Ambrose household. It went straight through the floor of it, because the floor was made of nothing else.

Down the slope from them, Corwin Tull kept a flock that any honest judge would call middling. Good enough, sound enough, but Corwin himself would tell you, if you caught him in a mood for honesty, that he had no particular gift with sheep, that he managed them competently the way a man manages a garden he did not plant himself. What Corwin had instead was a wife, Sela, who made cheese from the ewes' milk in spring and from a pair of cows they kept besides, and who had spent a decade building a name for it among the valley's households and even among the traders who came through, so that Tull cheese was asked for by name at more than one hearth I could name, mine among them. It was not a fortune, what the cheese brought in. Some years it was a modest sum indeed, barely worth the churning, Sela used to say, laughing at her own trade the way people laugh at things they secretly take great pride in. But it came from milk and rennet and patience, and none of it answered to the wool price at all. A trader in the lowland towns might decide wool was worth nothing that year, and the cheese would not hear of it, would not care, would sell at the same steady rate it always had, because people always want to eat and always want cheese on the table regardless of what fleece is fetching.

That autumn, when the wool buyers came up and named their poor price, Aldous Ambrose argued with them in the yard until his voice cracked, as though shouting might raise the market, and then he paid it, because there was no one else to sell to and the sheep needed shearing whether the price held or not, wool does not keep waiting on a man's pride. He came home that night and sat a long while at his table doing sums that would not come right no matter how he arranged them, and Ivet told me later, when enough years had passed that she could tell it plainly, that they had gone that whole winter without meat most weeks, had sold two good rams they ought to have kept for breeding just to see them through to spring, and had put off a debt to the miller that cost them more in the end than if they'd paid it on time. It was not ruin, quite. But it was the kind of year that leaves a mark on a family's face for a long while after, the kind of year Ivet still spoke of with a tightness in her jaw a decade on.

The Tulls, that same winter, ate as they always ate. Corwin's wool clip brought in half what it should have, same as everyone's, and he grumbled about it same as everyone did, standing in the common fold comparing his bad luck to his neighbors' the way men do when misery wants company. But Sela's cheese money came in steady as ever that year, because it had never had anything to do with wool in the first place, and between the two of them the household carried on much as it always had, no feast, no extravagance, but no hunger either, and no rams sold before their time.

I do not think Corwin was the wiser shepherd. I want to be honest about that, because it would be a tidier story if he were, and tidy stories are not always true ones. Aldous knew sheep better than Corwin ever would, bred better stock, culled more shrewdly, and in a fair year his flock earned more than the Tulls' ever did. But Aldous had built his whole house on one market's mood, and a market's mood is a thing no shepherd, however skilled, has ever governed. Sela's cheese was not cleverer than wool. It was simply a different thing entirely, answering to different hungers and different seasons of trade, so that when one failed the other did not fail with it, and that, I came to understand, is worth more some years than skill itself.

Ivet took up her carding again the spring after that hard winter, and this time Aldous did not call it thread money. He wrote it in the book, in his own hand, alongside the wool, and when I last saw that ledger, years later, there were two columns in it where once there had been one.

A household that draws every coin from a single market lives entirely at that market's mercy, however well it tends its flock. A second trade, answering to different hungers than the first, is not a distraction from the shepherd's work — it is the roof over it in the year the wool price falls.

CLOSING REFLECTION

I am an old woman now, and last spring a shepherd barely past his twentieth year stood at my tally-house door asking me which single story from this book mattered most, as if I kept a short version somewhere in a drawer that would save him the trouble of learning things the long way. He had that particular lean young men get when they're impatient—one shoulder against the frame, arms crossed, eyes already half-dismissing whatever I was about to say before I'd said it. I recognized it. I had stood in nearly that exact posture forty years earlier, in this same doorway, asking old Ossian the same question.

I should tell you to read all twenty-one stories, to sit with them, to let them settle into your bones over seasons rather than afternoons, because that's what actually works. Though I should say—and I mean this—I didn't do that myself. I read Ossian's first collection in a single night, cover to cover, then spent the next three years making exactly the mistakes he'd warned against, convinced each time that my situation was different enough to be exempt. It never was. The mountain asks the same questions of every generation, dressed up in new clothing, and every generation believes for a little while that the old answers don't apply to them. They always do. I just didn't want to wait to find that out, so I didn't, and I paid for the impatience in ways that still show up in my account books if you know where to look.

But here's what I've come to understand, keeping this valley's tallies for longer now than I care to count: you can hand someone the entire pattern of how fortunes are built and lost in a place like this, and most of them—not all, but most—will still have to learn it the hard way, one mistake at a time, because there's a gap between knowing a thing and believing it that can only be crossed by standing in the cold yourself, watching something you built fall apart because you didn't keep enough back. Knowing doesn't get you across that gap. Only the cold does.

I think about this every year at the autumn reckoning, when the whole valley gathers at the common fold and I read out the tallies—what each household gave into the common reserve, what they took out, what remains. There's always at least one family standing there who didn't contribute anything this year because the wool price was good and the season was easy and they couldn't see the point of setting money aside when they needed it right now for a better fence, or more stock, or a roof repair they'd been putting off. And I can see it on their faces, that thing young people have before they've lost anything big yet—that unearned certainty that next year will go at least as well as this one did, so there's no rush to build a reserve they may never need. They're polite about it. They nod when I read the numbers. But you can tell they think the old woman's being careful past the point of usefulness, and that the warnings in these twenty-one stories are meant for people less capable than they are.

Then winter comes.

Not every winter—that's the trick of it. Some years are mild, and those families skate through, and the lack of a reserve costs them nothing, and the lesson doesn't land. But every fourth or fifth winter, the mountain reminds us what it's actually capable of, and those are the years I get families standing at my door in February, faces tight, asking if there's anything left in the common reserve they can draw against, and if not, whether I know anyone who'll lend against next season's wool. And I do lend, when I can. Though I should say—I hate lending like that. I hate watching someone realize in real time that they're going to lose a flock, or a roof, or a season's income because they didn't believe the valley when it was trying to teach them something during the easy years. It's not satisfying to be proven right. It's just sad, mostly, and expensive for everyone, because a household that goes under doesn't just hurt itself—it weakens every household they owed money to, every household they would have bought from, every child who might have learned the work if the flock had still been there to learn it on.

That's the cost no one sees coming when they're twenty-three and standing at my door asking for the shortcut. They think the risk is theirs alone—that if they gamble and lose, it's only their own problem to solve. But a valley like this doesn't work that way. We're small enough and isolated enough that every household's fortune is knotted into every other household's in ways you can't see until someone pulls the thread too hard and three other families discover their stability was depending on that thread holding. Torvald Ren found that out the year his pasture collapsed and he couldn't pay the four families who'd sold him stock on credit. They found it out too. One of those families was mine, and I still remember my mother's face the night she realized Torvald's debt wasn't coming back, at least not that season, and we were going to have to make it through winter on a budget we'd built assuming that money would be there. We made it through. But it was closer than it should have been, and the whole problem traced back to one man's decision five years earlier to ignore the lesson about reserves because he thought he was competent enough not to need one.

You might be thinking, reading this, that I'm only trying to scare you into caution you don't need, that your situation genuinely is different, that these stories come from a time or a place that doesn't map cleanly onto wherever you're building your own fortune. Maybe. I can't see your valley from mine, so I can't say for certain. But I can tell you what I've watched happen across fifty years of keeping tallies in a place small enough that I've seen the whole of most families' financial lives from first flock to last: every single household that built something that lasted built it slowly, kept something back, and survived at least one season that should have ruined them but didn't, because they had a reserve they'd put aside during the years when it felt unnecessary. Every single household that collapsed collapsed fast—usually across a single season, sometimes a single month—and the collapse always traced back to a choice made years earlier, during a fat season, to spend or borrow or expand right up to the edge of what the good years could support, with nothing held back for the lean ones.

I know which pattern I want you to follow. Though I should say, I didn't follow it myself in my twenties, even after I'd read Ossian's stories, even after I'd watched my mother lose a season's income to Torvald's debt. I bought too much stock too young, on credit, because the wool price was climbing and I wanted to be the person who caught the wave while it was still building instead of the person who watched it from shore wishing they'd moved faster. I wasn't stupid. I'd run the numbers. The debt was manageable as long as the price held for two more seasons. It didn't hold for two more seasons. It broke in the spring, hard and fast, and I spent the next four years working that debt off while watching families who'd kept a reserve buy stock at the new low prices I couldn't afford anymore. I learned the lesson. I just learned it the way Ossian warned me I probably would—by ignoring the warning and paying for it later.

So I'm not standing here as someone who got it right the first time, or even the second time. I'm standing here as someone who got it wrong in most of the predictable ways, survived long enough to recognize the pattern I'd been living inside, and then spent the next thirty years watching other people step into the same traps wearing different boots, certain each time that their version of the mistake was different enough to be safe. It never was. The mountain's been asking the same questions since long before either of us was born, and it will keep asking them long after we're both gone, and your job—my job—anyone's job who wants to build something that outlasts a single lucky season—is just to recognize the shape of the question before you're standing fully inside the mistake with no good way out.

If you've read this far, you know by now that none of these twenty-one stories are actually about sheep. They never were. A flock is only ever the shape that wisdom wears when it's walking through a particular kind of country—mine happened to be high and cold and unforgiving, so my wisdom learned to speak in wool and hay and stone fences. Yours might be wearing an entirely different coat. But the underneath of it—the part about patience, about reserves, about telling the truth even when no one's checking, about building slowly and forgiving yourself the years it takes to see any of it pay off—that part, I think, is the same underneath in every valley that's ever kept a flock, or a coin, or a harvest, or anything else that grows if you tend it and vanishes if you don't.

There were more stories that reached me after the first edition went out—Tobin and Wick's lesson about borrowed stock, Torvald Ren's hard-won knowledge about common reserves, the smoke-fleece years that taught the whole valley what a fashion in wool costs when you stay too long. The Ambrose brothers and their overgrazed pasture. Tobin Ashgrove's handshake at the ford. Old Faron teaching his son to fail small. Sela Tull's quiet second trade that held when the wool price collapsed. They're all here now, set down alongside the rest, because I've come to think of this book less as a collection of individual lessons and more as a single long argument about what it actually takes to build something that lasts in a place that doesn't forgive carelessness. The argument is this: it takes longer than you want it to, it's less exciting than you hoped it would be, and every shortcut you're tempted to take will cost you more in the long run than the patience would have cost you up front. I know that's not the answer anyone wants. I didn't want it either. But it's the only answer

I've ever seen actually work, across five decades of tallies that don't lie.

Old Ossian told me once, the year I started keeping the valley's records, that I'd spend my whole life watching this valley make the same twenty-one mistakes in every generation, dressed up each time in new shepherd's clothing, believing each time that their circumstance was different enough to be exempt. "It never is," he said. "Your job isn't to stop the mistakes. No one's job is that. Your job is only to keep the stories where the next generation can find them, so that at least a few of them recognize the shape of the mistake before they're standing fully inside it." I thought at the time he was being pessimistic. Fifty years later, I think he was being exactly accurate, and I've come to believe that keeping the stories is enough—not because it prevents the mistakes, but because it shortens them, sometimes, by a season or two, for the people willing to look.

Here's what I'd ask you to carry away, if you're going to carry anything: every fortune worth having in this valley was built the same unglamorous way, one small, patient, mostly unwatched decision at a time. None of it arrived all at once. All of it could have been lost all at once—to a single winter, a single wager, a single afternoon of impatience—which is exactly why the patience mattered as much as it did. Build slowly. Keep something back. Tell the truth even when no one's checking. And forgive yourself the years it takes, because it will take years, and the valley has never once found a faster honest way.

The mountain doesn't care whether you understood any of this in time. It only asks, each season, the same plain question it's always asked: what did you build that can still stand when the snow comes. Answer that honestly, year after ordinary year, and the fortune tends to take care of itself.

I think often of my own mother, who kept a small flock on this same hillside before me and who told me once that the valley would go on asking the same questions of every shepherd who ever lived here, long after both of us were gone, and that this wasn't a discouraging thing to know but a steadying one. We're none of us the first to stand at a particular fence wondering whether to cull the ewe or carry her through winter, and none of us will be the last, and there's a kind of company in that, even in the seasons when no other person is standing beside you at the fence at all.

That young shepherd who came to my door last spring asking for the single story that mattered most—I didn't give him one. I told him what Ossian told me: read them all, slowly, more than once, and expect the reading to change as you get older, because the same story reads differently to someone who hasn't lost anything yet than it does to someone who has. He looked disappointed. I didn't blame him. I was disappointed too, forty years ago, standing in his boots, wanting the shortcut Ossian wouldn't give me. But I understand now why he didn't give it, and why I can't give it either. Wisdom doesn't live in any single story. It lives in the pattern all of them make together, the way a single thread tells you nothing about a bolt of cloth, but enough threads laid the same direction, season after season, tell you everything about the hand that wove it.

The autumn reckoning is next week. The whole valley will gather at the common fold—cider passed hand to hand, children weaving between the adults' legs, the year's tallies read out one household at a time. Somewhere in that circle will be a young shepherd who hasn't made any of the twenty-one mistakes in this book yet. They will, in time, make at least one of them, because that's what it means to be young and holding a fortune for the first time. But maybe—and this is the only reason I kept writing after the first edition, the only reason I'm still keeping tallies at an age when most women have handed the work to someone younger—maybe when the mistake arrives, some quiet corner of their memory will recognize its shape a season earlier than it would have on its own, and they'll reach for the reserve, or the honest scale, or the wall they should have built three years ago, just barely in time.

I can't promise that. But I've seen it happen, once or twice, across fifty years, and it's enough to keep the stories worth telling.

Also in the Series

Every book in Parable Wisdom stands on its own — read them in any order. If this one was useful, the library continues:

The Merchant's Ledger

The Weaver's Debt

The Glassblower's Gamble

The Miller's Measure

www.ingramcontent.com/pod-product-compliance
Lightning Source LLC
LaVergne TN
LVHW010722061126
851857LV00014B/1300
* 9 7 8 1 8 0 4 2 8 1 7 9 6 *